BREAKING FREE
OF
CODEPENDENCY

*A HOLISTIC GUIDE TO HEALING,
EMOTIONAL RESILIENCE, AND
SELF-EMPOWERMENT*

AMANDA TOLBER

Popoki Press, LLC

1st Edition
ISBN 979-8-30-625952-9

For my mother,

whose selflessness knows no bounds, unfortunately

CONTENTS

PART IV

PART V

PROLOGUE

IF YOU'VE PICKED UP THIS BOOK, you might be feeling a longing for change—a desire to find a way out of specific relationship patterns or emotional cycles that seem to hold you back. Maybe you've noticed how often you say "yes" when you'd rather say "no" or how you put others' needs above your own, hoping that, in return, you'll feel valued or loved. You might be caught in a loop of seeking approval yet feeling drained and resentful when it doesn't come. These shared experiences often point to a deeper, more complex pattern called codependency.

Codependency is a term that has gained considerable recognition over the years. It is commonly used to describe people who become overly focused on caring for others, often at the expense of their own needs. However, codependency is about more than just "caring too much"; it's an intricate pattern rooted in how we relate to ourselves, others, and the world. It often intertwines with issues like low self-worth, emotional dependence, and a deep-seated fear of rejection or abandonment.

As you read through this book, we'll also touch on two closely related dynamics that often accompany codependency: gaslighting and narcissistic abuse. Gaslighting is a form of manipulation that makes you question your reality, undermining your sense of self-trust and confidence. Narcissistic abuse, on the other hand, involves relationships where one person (often with narcissistic traits) exploits or controls another, feeding their need for validation at the other's expense. These patterns are all interconnected and can trap you in cycles of dependency, self-doubt, and emotional exhaustion.

This book offers a way forward—a holistic, practical guide to help you understand these patterns, break free from them, and create a life where you feel strong, whole, and valued.

How Codependency, Gaslighting, and Narcissistic Abuse Connect

Codependency, gaslighting, and narcissistic abuse often overlap in relationships, reinforcing each other in ways that can make you feel stuck or powerless. If you're codependent, you may naturally place others' needs above your own, looking for worth in how much you give or how needed you are. Narcissistic individuals, meanwhile, often crave attention and validation, and they can instinctively sense when someone is willing to provide this unconditionally. In such relationships, the codependent person may find themselves catering to the narcissistic person's demands, compromising their own well-being for the other's approval.

Gaslighting often creeps in here, too. When someone gaslights you, they manipulate your perception of reality, leading you to doubt your thoughts, feelings, and even your memories. A narcissistic partner might use gaslighting to maintain control, shifting blame onto you and minimizing your feelings or experiences. Over time, this erodes your confidence, making you increasingly dependent on the other person's version of reality. If you're codependent, you might already struggle to validate your feelings, and gaslighting intensifies this self-doubt, keeping you caught in a cycle where you feel unworthy and reliant on the approval of others.

Together, these dynamics form a web of emotional dependency that can be hard to recognize and even harder to break free from. This book is here to guide you in untangling these patterns and finding a way to heal. By understanding how codependency, gaslighting, and narcissistic abuse operate, you'll be able to recognize their signs in your own life and take steps to protect and honor your well-being.

Why This Book is Different

There are many books on codependency and self-help resources on toxic relationships, each with its own unique perspective and tools. This book, however, takes a holistic approach, combining scientifically grounded concepts with practical exercises to support you every step of the way. Here's how this book will be different:

1. Comprehensive Understanding

This book doesn't just focus on one part of the problem—it explores the full range of issues surrounding codependency, including its roots, the impact of family dynamics, and how cultural or societal factors can play a role. We'll also explore how trauma and early experiences may have shaped your patterns, providing a complete understanding of where codependency comes from and why it persists. This comprehensive approach will give you the knowledge and awareness you need to address all aspects of codependency, not just the symptoms.

2. Scientific Insights, Presented Simply

While codependency and narcissistic abuse can feel deeply personal and emotional, understanding their psychological roots can be incredibly empowering. This book presents insights from psychology and research in an accessible way so you can see how these patterns operate on both a personal and scientific level. You'll gain clarity on how codependency, gaslighting, and narcissistic abuse affect your brain, emotions, and self-perception. Understanding these processes helps demystify them, making it easier to approach healing with compassion and insight.

3. Practical Tools and Exercises

Awareness is the first step, but true transformation happens through action. Each chapter of this book includes practical exercises, reflective questions, and step-by-step guidance designed to help you apply what you're learning. These tools will empower you to begin setting boundaries, reclaiming your sense of self-worth, and developing resilience. Many of the exercises are applicable across several chapters but serve to both reinforce the lessons as well as allow you to selectively revisit any topic you find to be a personal weakness. By the end of the book, you'll have a toolkit filled with strategies to navigate relationships confidently, prioritize your own well-being, and live authentically.

4. Compassion, Not Judgment

Healing from codependency and toxic relationships is often a complex, emotional journey. It's easy to fall into self-blame or feel overwhelmed by the changes you're trying to make. This book is here to guide you with compassion, not judgment. There's no "perfect" way to heal, and each step you take is a victory. The goal is to support you in building a strong, nurturing relationship with yourself—a relationship that prioritizes self-love, patience, and kindness.

What You'll Gain from This Journey

This book is more than a guide to recognizing codependent patterns—it's an invitation to rediscover yourself, create boundaries that protect your well-being, and find the confidence to live according to your values. Here's what you can expect from the chapters ahead:

- A Deeper Understanding of Codependency and Its Origins: You'll explore how codependent tendencies develop, examining the influence of early relationships, family dynamics, and societal messages. This will help you see that these patterns aren't flaws or weaknesses—they're learned behaviors that you now have the power to change.

- Tools for Healing and Reclaiming Your Life: Through practical exercises, you'll learn to reconnect with your own needs, set boundaries, and release the need for external validation. These tools will help you develop emotional independence, cultivate self-worth, and create a foundation of inner strength.

- Strategies for Building Healthier Relationships: As you heal, you'll learn how to recognize supportive, balanced relationships while also developing the confidence to distance yourself from relationships that drain or harm you. You'll explore skills like assertive communication, conflict resolution, and healthy vulnerability, all of which allow you to engage in relationships from a place of strength.

- A Sense of Inner Freedom and Empowerment: The ultimate goal of this book is to help you live a life that reflects your true self. By breaking free from the need to please or seek approval, you'll create a truly fulfilling life, one where your choices align with your values, passions, and well-being.

Moving Forward

Healing from codependency, gaslighting, and narcissistic abuse is not a quick fix. It's a journey that requires courage, patience, and dedication. But as you work through this book, you'll have a supportive guide to help you untangle the layers of these patterns and build a life that reflects your worth, strength, and individuality.

Each chapter is here to equip you with knowledge, practical exercises, and compassionate guidance. It's designed to meet you where you are, with room to reflect, learn, and grow at your own pace. Take each chapter as it comes, allowing yourself to absorb the information, apply the exercises, and celebrate each step forward.

Remember that you're not alone. Millions of people have faced the challenges of codependency, and healing is entirely possible. This book is your companion on this journey, offering the tools, insights, and support to move you forward with confidence. By the end of this journey, you'll have built the foundations of a life rooted in self-love, resilience, and freedom—a life that reflects your true worth and authenticity.

Let's begin.

PART I

Chapter 1

Understanding Codependency

IF YOU'RE HERE, YOU MIGHT BE WONDERING what exactly codependency means. You may have heard the word in conversations, read about it online, or even recognized some of its traits in yourself or people close to you. Codependency is a term that can feel vague or even confusing, especially since it involves qualities that many people see as positive, like caring for others, being helpful, and wanting solid connections. But codependency goes beyond these qualities, involving a pattern of relationships and behaviors that, instead of enhancing well-being, often lead to emotional exhaustion, self-neglect, and a loss of identity.

In this chapter, we'll define what codependency truly is, look at how it differs from healthy dependency, and explore some real-life examples to bring this concept to life. By the end, you'll have a clearer understanding of what codependency looks like, how it can affect your life, and why recognizing it is the first step toward healing and building healthier relationships.

Defining Codependency

At its core, codependency is a pattern of behavior in which a person finds their sense of self-worth, purpose, and identity through caring for, helping, or fixing others. This can happen in any kind of relationship—romantic, familial, friendship, or even professional—but it most often shows up in close, emotionally significant relationships. The codependent person typically feels responsible for the other person's happiness, well-being, and emotional stability, often to the point of neglecting their own needs, desires, and boundaries.

Codependency often comes from a place of good intentions. People who struggle with codependency may genuinely want to help and support those they care about. However, these tendencies can spiral into a one-sided relationship where one person gives far more than they receive, sacrificing their own well-being to "keep the peace," prevent conflict, or gain approval. Over time, this dynamic can leave the codependent person feeling exhausted, resentful, and disconnected from their own sense of self.

Common signs of codependency include:

- Difficulty setting boundaries: Saying "no" feels uncomfortable or guilt-inducing.
- People-pleasing tendencies: Prioritizing others' happiness, even at the cost of your own.
- Fear of abandonment: Strong anxiety around being alone or losing relationships.
- Low self-worth: Feeling unworthy or inadequate unless helping or supporting someone else.
- Emotional over-investment: Feeling overly responsible for others' feelings and problems.

Codependency can look different for each person, but it generally involves a pattern of over-giving, sacrificing one's own needs, and relying on external sources for validation and self-worth. Let's look at a few real-life examples to make this clearer.

Real-Life Examples of Codependency

Understanding codependency can be easier when we see it in real-life scenarios. Here are some examples that highlight the different ways codependency can show up:

Example 1: The People-Pleasing Partner

Sharon has been in a relationship with her partner, Tom, for several years. She loves him deeply and wants him to be happy. Over time, Sarah has found herself saying "yes" to almost everything Tom asks for, even if it makes her uncomfortable or goes against her own needs. She rarely voices her desires or opinions, afraid it might lead to conflict or upset Tom. Sharon has gradually taken on most of the household responsibilities, doing everything possible to make life easier for Tom. But in the process, she feels drained, unseen, and unsupported.

Sharon's pattern is codependent because she prioritizes Tom's needs at the expense of her own, fearing that asserting herself might jeopardize their relationship. Her self-worth is tied to keeping Tom happy, even though it leaves her feeling depleted and unfulfilled.

Example 2: The Overly Responsible Sibling

Drew has a younger sister, Emily, who struggles with financial stability and frequently asks him for help. Drew cares deeply about Emily and wants to be there for her. Whenever she has a problem, Drew drops everything to assist, often giving her money, fixing her issues, or offering advice—even when it's inconvenient or stressful for him. Drew has come to feel responsible for Emily's happiness and success, to the point that he feels guilty if he can't help her right away.

Drew's codependent tendencies show up in his need to "fix" Emily's life, often at the expense of his own well-being. His sense of self-worth has become intertwined with being her helper, and he struggles to set boundaries, fearing that if he doesn't help, he's failing as a brother.

Example 3: The Self-Sacrificing Friend

Laura is known among her friends as "the rock." She's always available to listen to others' problems, provide advice, and lend a hand. While Laura is generous and compassionate, she rarely asks for help herself, even when she's struggling. She feels uncomfortable burdening her friends and worries they might pull away if she expresses her own needs. Over time, Laura feels emotionally drained and somewhat invisible, as if her worth depends entirely on being there for everyone else.

Laura's codependency is evident in her reluctance to receive support and her reliance on her role as the "helper" to feel valued. She finds it challenging to prioritize her own well-being, fearing that her friends won't value her if she doesn't give constantly.

Healthy Dependency vs. Codependency

It's important to recognize that not all forms of reliance or care for others are codependent. Relationships naturally involve a certain level of dependency, where both people lean on each other for support, connection, and companionship. This mutual dependency is a healthy part of human relationships and helps people feel connected, loved, and supported.

The difference between healthy dependency and codependency lies in the balance and boundaries within the relationship:

- **Healthy Dependency:** In a healthy, balanced relationship, both people support each other, and both are free to voice their needs, desires, and boundaries. Each person respects the other's individuality and independence. Dependency in this context means leaning on each other without feeling overly responsible for the other person's emotions or happiness. Both people maintain a sense of self and prioritize their well-being, trusting that the relationship is strong enough to withstand differences and personal boundaries.

- **Codependency:** In a codependent relationship, the balance is skewed. One person (or sometimes both) becomes overly focused on the other's needs, emotions, or approval to the detriment of their own well-being. Instead of mutual support, the relationship becomes one-sided, with the codependent person giving, sacrificing, and accommodating in ways that undermine their autonomy and sense of self. The codependent person feels responsible for "fixing" or "saving" the other person and may feel anxious or guilty when they focus on their own needs.

In a healthy relationship, both people can experience independence and interdependence. They know they're valued not just for what they give but for who they are. In a codependent relationship, however, worth becomes tied to what one can offer, do, or fix for the other, which can lead to burnout, resentment, and loss of identity.

Why Codependency Develops

Codependency doesn't appear out of nowhere; it often develops from patterns established in early relationships, family dynamics, or cultural expectations. For many, codependent tendencies began in childhood, where they might have learned that love and approval were earned by taking care of others, keeping the peace, or putting family members' needs above their own. In these situations, self-worth often becomes linked to how helpful or needed a person can be.

Family dynamics, such as growing up with a parent who was emotionally distant, critical, or dependent, can also contribute to codependency. Children in these environments may learn to over-compensate by becoming the "caretaker" in the family, often taking on adult responsibilities or trying to fix problems beyond their control.

Cultural or societal messages can reinforce these patterns. Certain roles, like being a "selfless" mother, a "supportive" spouse, or a "dependable" friend, are often celebrated to the point where self-care can be viewed as selfish or inappropriate. These beliefs can create pressure to fulfill these roles at the expense of one's own identity and happiness.

Recognizing Codependency in Yourself

Recognizing codependent patterns in yourself is the first step toward breaking free from them. Here are a few signs to help you reflect on your own tendencies:

1. Difficulty Saying "No": You often agree to requests, even when it's inconvenient or against your best interests, because you fear disappointing others.
2. Low Self-Worth: You find it difficult to feel valuable unless you're helping or supporting someone else, and you may feel unworthy on your own.

3. Fear of Rejection: You fear losing relationships or being alone if you don't constantly give, please, or support others.

4. Emotional Exhaustion: You feel drained, burned out, or resentful because you give so much to others without receiving enough in return.

5. Difficulty Asking for Help: You hesitate to ask for help or support, feeling that your role is to provide, not receive, care.

If any of these signs resonate with you, know that you're not alone. Many people struggle with codependent patterns, often without realizing it, and the fact that you're reading this book shows that you're ready to make positive changes.

Moving Forward

Understanding codependency and how it differs from healthy dependency is an essential first step. Recognizing these patterns allows you to take a step back and evaluate your relationships, not from a place of self-blame but from a place of compassion. Codependency doesn't make you weak or flawed; it's simply a pattern that developed over time, often out of a desire to connect, be loved, or feel secure.

In the chapters to come, we'll explore the roots of codependency, look at how early experiences shaped these patterns, and begin the work of unlearning behaviors that no longer serve you. Through practical tools, exercises, and reflections, you'll learn to develop healthy boundaries, build self-worth, and create balanced, fulfilling relationships.

Your journey starts here, and every insight you gain brings you closer to the freedom, strength, and authenticity waiting on the other side of codependency.

Chapter 2

The Origins of Codependency

CODEPENDENCY IS OFTEN DESCRIBED AS A PATTERN of behavior that's learned over time. People aren't born with codependent tendencies; they develop them based on their relationships, experiences, and the environments in which they grew up. Understanding where codependency originates is crucial for breaking free from it. When you can recognize the root causes, it becomes easier to understand why these patterns exist in your life and how you can begin to change them.

In this chapter, we'll explore the key factors contributing to codependency, starting with family dynamics and attachment styles. We'll also examine how dysfunctional relationships, abuse, and trauma can foster codependent behaviors, as well as the role that cultural and societal expectations play in reinforcing these patterns. By gaining insight into the origins of codependency, you'll be better equipped to approach your healing journey with empathy and clarity.

Family Dynamics and Attachment Styles

Our earliest relationships, especially with our caregivers, play a significant role in shaping how we relate to others and to ourselves. As children, we look to our caregivers for love, support, and guidance, and the way these needs are met influences our beliefs about worth, safety, and relationships. For many people who develop codependent tendencies, these early relationships were marked by inconsistent care, emotional unavailability, or a need to fulfill a particular role to receive love.

Attachment Styles and Their Role in Codependency

Psychologists have identified four primary attachment styles: secure, anxious, avoidant, and disorganized. These styles reflect different ways of relating to others based on early experiences with caregivers:

- **Secure Attachment:** In secure attachments, caregivers are generally responsive and consistent, which helps children develop a strong sense of self-worth and trust in others. People with secure attachment styles tend to form healthy, balanced relationships as adults.
- **Anxious Attachment:** When caregivers are inconsistent—sometimes available and sometimes distant—children can develop an anxious attachment style. They may grow up feeling insecure, often seeking approval and fearing rejection. This need for constant reassurance can lead to codependent behaviors, as they feel that their worth depends on being needed or accepted by others.
- **Avoidant Attachment:** Children who grow up with emotionally unavailable caregivers may develop what is known as an avoidant attachment style, learning to suppress their needs and emotions. While avoidant individuals are less likely to exhibit overt codependent behaviors, they may strug-

gle to connect emotionally, making it difficult for them to form healthy, interdependent relationships.

- **Disorganized Attachment:** In cases where caregivers are abusive or unpredictable, children may develop a disorganized attachment style. This style involves a mix of anxious and avoidant tendencies, often leading to a deep-seated fear of intimacy combined with a craving for connection. Disorganized attachment is frequently associated with codependent patterns, as individuals struggle with both a fear of abandonment and a mistrust of closeness.

If you find yourself identifying with anxious or disorganized attachment styles, it may be a clue to understanding the roots of codependency in your life. Recognizing these patterns allows you to approach them with compassion, knowing that they developed as a way to cope with the care you received as a child.

Family Roles and Codependency

In families where codependency is present, specific roles often emerge, shaping how individuals see themselves and interact with others. Common roles include:

- **The Caretaker:** This person feels responsible for everyone else's well-being and often neglects their own needs. They may have learned early on that love is earned through self-sacrifice and caretaking.
- **The Hero:** The hero is the person who takes on adult responsibilities or excels to compensate for family instability. They often believe their worth comes from achievements or being "strong" for others.

- **The Peacemaker:** The peacemaker tries to keep everyone calm, often avoiding conflict and setting aside their own feelings to maintain harmony. They may feel uncomfortable asserting themselves, fearing it will disrupt family peace.

These roles can persist into adulthood, creating a tendency to prioritize others, avoid conflict, and seek self-worth in external sources. If you recognize any of these roles in yourself, it can be helpful to reflect on how they may have shaped your current relationships.

The Impact of Dysfunctional Relationships, Abuse, and Trauma

In addition to family dynamics, experiences of abuse or trauma can profoundly impact how we relate to others and to ourselves. Trauma doesn't always have to be a single, catastrophic event; it can also include ongoing experiences of neglect, emotional abuse, or invalidation. These experiences can leave lasting effects on self-worth, trust, and the ability to set healthy boundaries.

Emotional and Psychological Trauma

Emotional trauma can stem from various sources, such as living with a critical parent, being subjected to bullying, or experiencing repeated invalidation of your feelings. When children are consistently told that their emotions don't matter or are exaggerated, they may learn to ignore or suppress their feelings. This can lead to codependent tendencies, as they start to seek validation externally rather than trusting their own perceptions and emotions.

For instance, if you were often told as a child to "get over it" or "stop being so sensitive," you might have learned to silence your emotions in relationships, focusing on others' needs while neglecting your own. This creates a pattern where you may become overly attuned to others' feelings, seeking to manage or fix them to gain acceptance.

Physical and Sexual Trauma

Experiences of physical or sexual trauma can also lead to codependent behaviors. Survivors of such trauma often struggle with boundaries, as their boundaries were violated in deeply painful ways. This can create a tendency to ignore one's own limits or feel responsible for others' feelings, as a way to maintain control and avoid conflict.

For example, if you grew up in a home where physical boundaries were regularly crossed, you might find it challenging to assert yourself or say "no" as an adult. You may feel compelled to please others, believing that doing so will protect you from further pain or rejection.

Intellectual and Psychological Manipulation

Intellectual abuse or manipulation, such as gaslighting, can distort a person's sense of reality, making them question their thoughts and feelings. When someone is repeatedly told that their perceptions are "wrong" or "crazy," they can lose trust in their own judgment. This can lead to codependency, as they begin to rely on others for validation and decision-making, doubting their own ability to make choices.

Gaslighting, a form of psychological manipulation, is often used in narcissistic relationships to keep the codependent person feeling insecure and dependent. Over time, this can erode self-trust and reinforce the belief that one's worth is tied to pleasing or placating others.

Societal and Cultural Contributions to Codependent Behaviors

In addition to family and personal experiences, societal and cultural expectations can reinforce codependent behaviors, often in subtle but powerful ways. Many cultures emphasize self-sacrifice, loyalty, and service to others, particularly within certain roles, like being a parent, spouse, or close friend. While these values can promote strong community bonds, they can also create pressure to ignore one's own needs and prioritize others at all costs.

Gender Expectations

Gender norms and expectations often play a role in codependency, especially for women, who are frequently socialized to be nurturing, supportive, and self-sacrificing. Messages like "put others first" or "good women don't complain" can reinforce the belief that one's worth is measured by how much one gives or sacrifices for others. This can lead to difficulty setting boundaries, as it feels "wrong" or "selfish" to prioritize personal needs.

Men, on the other hand, may be socialized to suppress their emotions, value stoicism, and take on roles as providers or "fixers." This can also lead to codependency, especially if they feel their worth is tied to solving others' problems or maintaining control in relationships. These expectations can create a sense of responsibility for others' happiness or well-being, reinforcing codependent patterns.

Cultural Values and Family Loyalty

In some cultures, loyalty to family and community is highly valued, and family needs are expected to be prioritized above personal desires. While this value can create strong support systems, it can also make it difficult for individuals to set boundaries, pursue personal goals, or detach from toxic relationships. In these contexts, saying "no" or prioritizing oneself may feel like a betrayal, creating internal conflict and reinforcing codependent tendencies.

The Media and Social Messages

The media often portrays self-sacrifice, martyrdom, and people-pleasing as virtuous traits, especially in certain roles. Movies, shows, and advertisements frequently glorify individuals who give everything for others, even at their own expense. These messages can subtly reinforce the idea that being "good" means being selfless and ignoring one's own needs, creating a societal backdrop that normalizes codependent behaviors.

By understanding the cultural and societal factors contributing to codependency, you can see how deeply ingrained these patterns can be. Recognizing these influences allows you to approach them with awareness, question whether these expectations truly serve your well-being, and align your actions with your own values.

Reflecting on the Origins of Your Codependent Patterns

As you consider the various factors that contribute to codependency, take a moment to reflect on your own experiences. Which of these influences resonate with you? Did your family dynamics, attachment style, or early experiences shape how you relate to others? Are there societal or cultural messages that make it difficult for you to set boundaries or prioritize yourself?

Understanding where your codependent tendencies come from isn't about placing blame; it's about gaining insight. These patterns developed as a way to cope with difficult experiences, fulfill social expectations, or create a sense of safety in challenging situations. But now, you have the opportunity to reassess these patterns and choose a different path—one that prioritizes your well-being and allows you to live authentically.

Moving Forward

By examining the origins of codependency, you're taking an essential step toward healing. You're beginning to see that codependency is not a "flaw" or personal failure but rather a learned pattern that developed in response to complex factors. This understanding allows you to approach yourself with empathy, acknowledging the influences that shaped you and creating space for change.

In the next chapter, we'll explore another key aspect of codependency: recognizing narcissistic and gaslighting behaviors. These dynamics often reinforce codependent patterns, making it challenging to break free. By understanding these behaviors, you'll be better equipped to protect your boundaries and assert your self-worth. Each chapter is here to support you in building a life of balance, strength, and self-respect—one step at a time.

Chapter 3

Recognizing Narcissistic & Gaslighting Behaviors

AS YOU CONTINUE YOUR JOURNEY TOWARD UNDERSTANDING and healing from codependency, it's important to recognize two patterns that often intertwine with it: narcissism and gaslighting. Many people who struggle with codependency find themselves in relationships where narcissistic and gaslighting behaviors are present, making it difficult to break free from cycles of dependency and low self-worth. These behaviors can undermine your confidence, create self-doubt, and trap you in dynamics that compromise your well-being.

In this chapter, we'll explore what narcissistic and gaslighting behaviors look like, explain the tactics commonly used in these re-lationships, and outline some of the red flags that indicate you may be dealing with psychological manipulation. By understanding these patterns, you'll be better equipped to protect yourself, recognize un-healthy dynamics, and begin to establish boundaries that honor your self-worth.

What is Narcissism?

Narcissism, as a term, is often used loosely to describe people who seem self-centered, arrogant, or overly focused on themselves. While everyone has moments of self-interest, true narcissistic behavior goes beyond occasional selfishness or vanity. Narcissistic Personality Disorder (NPD) is a recognized mental health condition characterized by having a persistent need for admiration, having a lack of empathy, and holding a strong sense of entitlement. Not everyone who displays narcissistic behaviors has NPD, but certain traits associated with narcissism can lead to toxic relationship dynamics.

Narcissistic individuals often believe they are superior to others, requiring constant admiration and validation to feel secure. This need can lead them to manipulate, control, or exploit others to meet their own emotional needs. Relationships with narcissists can be challenging because the narcissist often disregards or invalidates the other person's feelings, focusing only on what benefits them.

Key Traits of Narcissistic Individuals

- **Grandiosity and Self-Importance:** Narcissistic individuals often have an inflated sense of their own importance, achievements, or abilities. They may expect special treatment or feel entitled to certain privileges.

- **Lack of Empathy:** Empathy is the ability to understand and share the feelings of others. Narcissists struggle with this, often dismissing or minimizing others' emotions. They may ignore your needs and fail to show genuine concern or compassion.

- **Constant Need for Admiration:** Narcissists often rely on external validation to feel good about themselves. They may demand praise, recognition, or approval and become irritable or withdrawn if they don't receive it.

- **Manipulative Behavior:** Narcissists often use manipulation to maintain control in relationships. They may use tactics like gaslighting, guilt-tripping, or giving "conditional love" to keep others focused on their needs.

- **Envy and Jealousy:** Narcissists can be envious of others' success, appearance, or accomplishments and may try to undermine or belittle others to feel superior.

Red Flags of Narcissistic Behavior in Relationships

Recognizing narcissistic behaviors early on can help you set boundaries and protect yourself from being drawn into toxic dynamics. Here are some common red flags:

1. **Love Bombing:** At the beginning of a relationship, a narcissist may "love bomb" their partner, showering them with attention, praise, and affection. This intense focus can feel flattering, but it often serves to create dependency, making you feel special and indebted to them.

2. **Self-Centered Conversations:** Narcissists often dominate conversations, steering them back to themselves. They may seem disinterested or dismissive when you talk about your experiences or feelings, shifting the focus back to their own interests or concerns.

3. **Exaggerated Achievements:** They may constantly bring up their accomplishments or exaggerate their successes, seeking admiration and validation. They may also dismiss or downplay your achievements.

4. **Emotional Manipulation:** Narcissists may use guilt, fear, or manipulation to control you. For example, they might imply that you don't care enough about them if you don't do what they want or guilt you into prioritizing their needs

over yours.

5. **Idealization and Devaluation Cycle:** Narcissists often go through cycles of idealizing and devaluing others. Initially, they might place you on a pedestal, praising you and making you feel special. But when their interest wanes or their needs aren't met, they may suddenly withdraw or become critical, leaving you feeling confused and hurt.

6. **Gaslighting and Blame Shifting:** Narcissistic individuals frequently engage in gaslighting (discussed in detail below) and blame-shifting, taking no responsibility for their actions and making you question your own perceptions.

Understanding these red flags can help you identify narcissistic behaviors in relationships and, ultimately, make informed choices about who you allow into your life.

Understanding Gaslighting

Gaslighting is a form of psychological manipulation where someone tries to make you doubt your own reality, memory, or perceptions. The term stems from the 1938 play Gas Light, where a husband manipulates his wife into questioning her sanity by dimming their home's gas lights and then denying it happened. Gaslighting tactics can be subtle or overt, but the goal is to create self-doubt and confusion, making the other person feel dependent and insecure.

Gaslighting often occurs in relationships with narcissistic individuals or others who seek control, as it allows them to undermine your confidence, making it easier to manipulate you. Over time, gaslighting can lead to severe emotional and psychological effects, including anxiety, depression, and a loss of self-trust.

Common Gaslighting Tactics

- **Denying or Dismissing Feelings:** A gaslighter may dismiss or belittle your feelings, saying things like, "You're overreacting" or "You're too sensitive." This may make you question whether your emotions are valid.

- **Withholding Information:** The gaslighter might intentionally withhold information or deny things they previously said, creating a sense of uncertainty and confusion.

- **Countering:** When you bring up an event or express your feelings, the gaslighter may contradict you, saying things like, "That never happened," or "You're remembering it wrong." This tactic is designed to make you doubt your memory and perception.

- **Diverting or Distracting:** Gaslighters often deflect responsibility by changing the subject or diverting attention to unrelated issues, avoiding accountability and keeping you off-balance.

- **Trivializing:** The gaslighter may minimize your thoughts, experiences, or achievements to make you feel small or unimportant. For example, they might say, "That's not a big deal," or "You're making this up in your head."

- **Blame Shifting:** Gaslighters often turn the tables, making you feel responsible for their actions. For instance, if they've acted inappropriately, they may say, "I wouldn't have done that if you hadn't provoked me," or "You're the reason I reacted that way."

Effects of Gaslighting on Self-Worth and Mental Health

Gaslighting can have profound effects on mental health and self-esteem. When someone constantly questions your reality, you begin to doubt your own judgment, feelings, and perceptions. You may feel like you can't trust yourself and become increasingly dependent on the gaslighter for "clarity." Over time, gaslighting can lead to:

- **Confusion:** You may find it difficult to distinguish between reality and manipulation, leading to constant self-doubt.
- **Self-Doubt:** Gaslighting erodes confidence, making you question your own decisions and feelings.
- **Loss of Self-Trust:** You may lose trust in your own intuition, relying instead on others to validate your experiences.
- **Anxiety and Depression:** The psychological effects of gaslighting can lead to chronic anxiety, feelings of worthlessness, and depression.

Manipulation and Control Tactics in Abusive Relationships

Narcissistic and gaslighting behaviors often come with other manipulation tactics that keep you emotionally entangled and undermine your autonomy. Recognizing these tactics can help you set boundaries and protect your mental health.

Common Manipulation and Control Tactics

1. **Isolation:** Manipulative individuals often try to isolate you from friends, family, or supportive people in your life. They may create tension between you and others, making you feel increasingly dependent on them.
2. **Guilt-Tripping:** Guilt is a powerful tool in controlling someone's behavior. Manipulative people may guilt-trip you by making you feel selfish or uncaring if you don't meet their demands, reinforcing their control.

3. **Playing the Victim:** Narcissistic individuals often play the victim, especially when you try to set boundaries or assert yourself. They may portray themselves as misunderstood or mistreated, making you feel guilty for prioritizing your needs.

4. **Gaslighting through Triangulation:** Triangulation involves including a third party into the relationship dynamic to create emotional upheaval in the forms of jealousy, rivalry, or insecurity. For example, a narcissistic person may compare you to someone else or bring others into personal conflicts, making you feel off-balance.

5. **Silent Treatment:** The silent treatment is a type of emotional manipulation where the narcissist withholds communication to "punish" you or make you feel ignored. This tactic creates anxiety, making you feel compelled to win back their attention or approval.

6. **Conditional Love:** Conditional love is when someone gives affection or attention only when you behave in ways they approve of. This makes you feel that love and acceptance are dependent on meeting their expectations, reinforcing codependent behaviors.

Red Flags and Protecting Yourself

Understanding the tactics used in narcissistic and gaslighting behaviors is essential for protecting yourself and setting boundaries. Here are some red flags to watch for and steps you can take to protect yourself:

Red Flags of Manipulation and Control

*   Constantly feeling confused or "off-balance" in the rela-

tionship
- Feeling like you're "walking on eggshells" to avoid conflict
- Regularly questioning your own perceptions or memory
- Feeling responsible for the other person's happiness or anger
- Frequent cycles of affection followed by withdrawal or criticism

Steps for Protection and Self-Care

1. **Trust Your Instincts:** If something feels "off" in a relationship, trust that feeling. Manipulative people often create doubt, but your intuition is a powerful guide.

2. **Set Clear Boundaries:** Boundaries are essential for protecting your mental health. Communicate your limits firmly and stick to them, even if the other person tries to challenge or manipulate you.

3. **Seek Support:** Isolation is a common tactic in manipulative relationships. Reach out to friends, family, or support groups to gain perspective and strength. Trusted friends and a support network can remind you of your worth and help you see the relationship clearly.

4. **Educate Yourself:** Knowledge is power. The more you understand about narcissistic behaviors and gaslighting, the better equipped you'll be to recognize and respond to these tactics.

5. **Consider Professional Help:** Dealing with a narcissistic or manipulative person can be incredibly challenging. A therapist or counselor can provide valuable support and guidance, helping you develop strategies for coping, setting boundaries, and building self-worth.

Moving Forward

Recognizing narcissistic and gaslighting behaviors is a powerful step toward reclaiming your autonomy and building healthy, balanced relationships. These dynamics can be confusing and damaging, but with knowledge and awareness, you can protect yourself and set the foundation for healthier connections. Remember, you deserve relationships that honor your boundaries, respect your emotions, and support your well-being.

In the next chapter, we'll focus on building self-awareness and breaking free from codependent patterns. Through reflective exercises and practical tools, you'll learn to recognize your own emotional needs, strengthen your sense of self, and take the next steps toward lasting healing and personal growth.

Chapter 4

The Psychology of Trauma & PTSD

IN UNDERSTANDING AND HEALING FROM CODEPENDENCY, it's essential to recognize the impact of trauma. Trauma, especially when it occurs over long periods or during formative years, can fundamentally shape how we see ourselves, how we relate to others, and how we experience emotions. Many people who struggle with codependency or find themselves in toxic relationships may have experienced trauma that has altered their sense of self-worth, ability to trust, and capacity for emotional regulation.

This chapter explores the psychological and physiological effects of trauma, with a focus on complex PTSD (C-PTSD). This condition often arises from prolonged, repeated trauma, such as emotional abuse, neglect, or manipulation. We'll look at how trauma impacts the brain, body, and relationships, helping you gain insight into the deeper layers of healing. Trauma does not define you, but understanding its effects can be the first step toward reclaiming your sense of peace, self-worth, and emotional freedom.

Understanding Complex PTSD (C-PTSD) and Its Symptoms

While many people are familiar with PTSD (Post-Traumatic Stress Disorder), which often results from a single traumatic event, complex PTSD (C-PTSD) is a form of trauma that arises from prolonged exposure to traumatic situations, especially those involving emotional or physical abuse, neglect, or control. C-PTSD is commonly seen in In understanding and healing from codependency, it's essential to recognize the impact of trauma. Trauma, especially when it occurs over long periods or during formative years, can fundamentally shape how we see ourselves, how we relate to others, and how we experience emotions. Many people who struggle with codependency or find themselves in toxic relationships may have experienced trauma that has altered their sense of self-worth, ability to trust, and capacity for emotional regulation.

This chapter explores the psychological and physiological effects of trauma, with a focus on complex PTSD (C-PTSD). This condition often arises from prolonged, repeated trauma, such as emotional abuse, neglect, or manipulation. We'll look at how trauma impacts the brain, body, and relationships, helping you gain insight into the deeper layers of healing. Trauma does not define you, but understanding its effects can be the first step toward reclaiming your sense of peace, self-worth, and emotional freedom.

Understanding Complex PTSD (C-PTSD) and Its Symptoms

While many people are familiar with PTSD (Post-Traumatic Stress Disorder), which often results from a single traumatic event, complex PTSD (C-PTSD) is a form of trauma that arises from prolonged exposure to traumatic situations, especially those involving emotional or physical abuse, neglect, or control. C-PTSD is commonly seen in individuals who have endured ongoing trauma, such as in childhood or abusive relationships.

Key Symptoms of C-PTSD

C-PTSD has several symptoms that can profoundly impact a person's life. Here are some of the most common:

- **Negative Self-Perception:** People with C-PTSD often struggle with feelings of worthlessness, guilt, and shame. They may see themselves as inherently "flawed" or "bad," leading to low self-esteem and self-worth.

- **Emotional Dysregulation:** Emotional regulation is the ability to manage emotions in a balanced way. Those with C-PTSD may experience intense mood swings, feelings of sadness or anger that seem to come out of nowhere, and difficulty calming themselves.

- **Hypervigilance and Anxiety:** C-PTSD often leads to a state of hypervigilance, where individuals feel constantly "on edge" or fearful, always waiting for something to go wrong. This anxiety can be exhausting and make it challenging to relax.

- **Avoidance of Intimacy:** Relationships can feel overwhelming or unsafe for those with C-PTSD. Many people with C-PTSD struggle with intimacy, either withdrawing from closeness or engaging in relationships that repeat the dynamics of their trauma.

- **Difficulty Trusting Others:** Trauma can erode trust in others, making it difficult for people with C-PTSD to rely on or connect with others. They may fear betrayal, rejection, or abandonment, leading to codependent behaviors as they try to "secure" relationships.

- **Re-enactment of Trauma:** Sometimes, people with C-PTSD unconsciously recreate or seek out situations that resemble their original trauma. This can lead to a cycle of toxic or abusive relationships where familiar dynamics feel safe or "normal."

Understanding these symptoms is an essential first step in recognizing how trauma has shaped your experiences. It's not about blaming yourself for your behaviors; instead, it's about understanding the effects of trauma and acknowledging that these patterns are a natural response to prolonged distress.

How Trauma Impacts Self-Perception, Emotional Regulation, and Relationships

Trauma, especially when it occurs early in life or over a prolonged period, fundamentally alters the way we perceive ourselves and interact with others. Let's explore how trauma affects three core aspects of our being: self-perception, emotional regulation, and relationships.

Self-Perception

Trauma can leave deep emotional scars on a person's sense of self. Individuals who experience prolonged trauma, especially in relationships with significant figures (such as parents, caregivers, or partners), often internalize negative messages about themselves. They may come to believe they are unworthy, "bad," or somehow responsible for the abuse they endured.

For example, a child who grows up with a critical or emotionally abusive parent might learn to believe that they're only lovable if they're perfect, quiet, or accommodating. As an adult, they might carry these beliefs into relationships, feeling the need to over-give, people-please, or avoid conflict to maintain others' approval. This low self-worth can feed into codependent patterns, where a person's sense of value depends on others' approval or validation.

Emotional Regulation

Trauma disrupts the body's natural ability to regulate emotions. In healthy emotional regulation, the brain and body work together to manage stress, sadness, joy, and other feelings in a balanced way. However, trauma disrupts this process, leading to emotional dys-regulation—a state where emotions feel overwhelming, intense, and difficult to control.

People with trauma may find themselves struggling with sudden outbursts, prolonged sadness, or anger that feels disproportionate to the situation. They may also experience "emotional numbing," where feelings seem muted or inaccessible as a way to protect themselves from pain. This emotional dysregulation can make relationships challenging, as the individual may struggle to communicate their feelings or respond calmly in stressful situations.

Relationships

Trauma can also significantly impact how a person forms and maintains relationships. People with trauma often find themselves in one of two extremes: either overly dependent on relationships or fearful of intimacy altogether. This ambivalence often stems from early attachment experiences, where trust, safety, and connection were compromised.

For example, someone who has experienced emotional neglect may feel an intense need for closeness, fearing abandonment or rejection. This can lead to codependent behaviors, where they place others' needs above their own to maintain a sense of security. Conversely, someone with a history of betrayal may struggle to trust others, keeping people at arm's length to protect themselves from further harm. Both responses are protective but can lead to challenges in forming healthy, balanced relationships.

How Trauma Affects the Brain and Body

Understanding the science behind trauma can be empowering, as it helps to demystify why certain patterns or responses occur. Trauma affects both the brain and the body in profound ways, and these changes can impact everything from emotional regulation to physical health. Here, we'll explore some key ways trauma shapes the brain and body, highlighting how these effects relate to codependent behaviors and emotional challenges.

The Role of the Amygdala: The Brain's "Alarm System"

The amygdala is a small part of the brain that plays a crucial role in detecting threats and triggering the body's "fight-or-flight" response. When we experience trauma, the amygdala becomes hypersensitive, leading to a heightened state of alertness or hypervigilance. For someone with trauma, the amygdala may react to everyday situations as if they're threatening, causing anxiety, fear, and an inability to relax.

In relationships, this hypervigilance can manifest as fear of abandonment, rejection, or criticism. A person may become overly focused on others' needs or behaviors, constantly monitoring the relationship to prevent perceived threats. This can lead to codependent behaviors, as the person tries to maintain control or stability to feel safe.

The Hippocampus: Memory and Trauma

The hippocampus, a brain region involved in memory and emotional processing, is also affected by trauma. Trauma can alter the functioning of the hippocampus, making it difficult for people to accurately recall events or process their emotions. In some cases, traumatic memories become fragmented or suppressed, leading to gaps in memory or difficulty integrating past experiences.

This disruption can lead to confusion, as individuals with trauma may struggle to make sense of their feelings or understand why certain situations trigger intense emotions. These memory disruptions can also create vulnerability in relationships, where gaslighting or manipulation tactics exacerbate self-doubt. In a codependent dynamic, a person with trauma might find it challenging to trust their own memory or perceptions, increasing their reliance on external validation.

The Prefrontal Cortex: Decision-Making and Impulse Control

The prefrontal cortex, responsible for impulse control, decision-making, and rational thought, is another brain area impacted by trauma. Chronic trauma can impair the prefrontal cortex, making it difficult for people to make balanced decisions or respond thoughtfully in stressful situations. Instead, they may feel overwhelmed, reactive, or impulsive.

In relationships, this difficulty with decision-making and impulse control can lead to codependent behaviors, where a person struggles to set boundaries or act in their best interest. They may find it hard to say "no" or prioritize their own needs, fearing conflict or the possibility of losing the relationship.

Trauma and the Body: The Role of the Nervous System

In addition to affecting the brain, trauma has a profound impact on the body, especially the nervous system. Trauma triggers a state of "fight, flight, or freeze" in the nervous system, creating physical symptoms that can linger long after the traumatic experience has ended.

Chronic Stress and Physical Health

Prolonged trauma can lead to chronic activation of the body's stress response, resulting in issues like muscle tension, digestive problems, headaches, and fatigue. This chronic stress strains the body, weakening the immune system and increasing the risk of illnesses. People with trauma often experience physical symptoms like stomachaches, headaches, or insomnia, which can become chronic if left unaddressed.

Hyperarousal and Hypoarousal: Finding Balance

Trauma can create a pattern of hyperarousal (feeling overly alert and reactive) or hypoarousal (feeling numb or disconnected). Hyperarousal can lead to heightened anxiety, while hypoarousal can create feelings of emotional numbness. People with trauma may swing between these states, struggling to find a balanced, calm state of being.

In relationships, these states can make it challenging to engage in healthy ways. Hyperarousal might cause someone to feel anxious and fearful, making them overly reliant on their partner, while hypoarousal can lead to emotional withdrawal or difficulty connecting. These extremes create instability, reinforcing the cycle of codependent behaviors as the person seeks external sources of stability.

Moving Forward: Recognizing Trauma's Impact on Your Life

Understanding how trauma affects the mind, body, and emotions allows you to approach your healing journey with compassion and clarity. The effects of trauma are not flaws or weaknesses; they are natural responses to overwhelming experiences. Recognizing these effects can help you approach your patterns with empathy, understanding that these behaviors developed as a way to survive difficult situations.

Healing from trauma involves reconnecting with your sense of self, learning to regulate emotions, and building resilience. By recognizing the impact of trauma, you empower yourself to take steps toward healing, creating a foundation of inner strength and self-worth.

Next Steps: Healing and Reclaiming Your Life

In the next chapter, we'll begin exploring tools and practices for cultivating self-awareness and breaking free from codependent patterns. By reconnecting with your own needs, understanding your triggers, and building a foundation of self-compassion, you'll begin to heal from the effects of trauma and codependency. Remember, this journey is a process, and each step you take brings you closer to a life of peace, resilience, and freedom.

PART II

Chapter 5

Cultivating Self-Awareness

ONE OF THE MOST TRANSFORMATIVE STEPS IN overcoming codependency is developing self-awareness. Self-awareness is the ability to understand your own emotions, thoughts, and behaviors, serving as the foundation for lasting change. By becoming more self-aware, you can start to recognize your codependent patterns, understand what triggers your emotional responses, and begin to cultivate a sense of self that is independent of others' needs or approval.

In this chapter, we'll explore practical exercises to help you identify codependent behaviors, recognize your personal triggers, and build a deeper understanding of your emotional responses. Developing a healthy sense of self will empower you to make choices based on your own needs and values rather than relying on external validation. This process is an essential step toward creating a fulfilling, balanced life and forming supportive, respectful, and mutually enriching relationships.

Identifying Codependent Behaviors and Patterns

To break free from codependency, it's essential to identify specific behaviors that may be holding you back. Codependent patterns can be subtle and deeply ingrained, often going unnoticed in our daily lives. By shining a light on these patterns, you'll gain clarity on the ways in which they impact your relationships and well-being.

Common Codependent Behaviors

Here are some of the most common codependent behaviors. As you read through them, reflect on whether any of these resonate with your own experiences:

- **People-Pleasing:** Prioritizing others' needs and happiness over your own, often out of fear of disappointing them.
- **Difficulty Setting Boundaries:** Struggling to say "no" or feeling guilty when you assert your needs.
- **Fear of Abandonment:** Experiencing anxiety about being left alone or rejected, which may lead you to overextend yourself in relationships.
- **Low Self-Worth:** Feeling that your value is tied to how much you do for others or how well you fulfill their needs.
- **Over-Involvement in Others' Problems:** Taking on others' problems as your own, often feeling responsible for fixing them.
- **Neglecting Personal Needs:** Ignoring or suppressing your own needs, emotions, or desires to keep others happy.

These behaviors are not "bad" or shameful; they are simply coping mechanisms that you developed over time. Recognizing them is the first step in understanding how they may be limiting your growth and happiness.

Exercise: Identifying Your Codependent Patterns

This exercise is designed to help you reflect on your codependent tendencies and become more aware of how they show up in your relationships.

1. **Reflect on Past Relationships:** Think about significant relationships in your life, whether with family members, friends, or romantic partners. Consider the following questions:

- Did I feel responsible for their happiness or well-being?
- Did I often put their needs before my own?
- Did I have difficulty asserting myself or setting boundaries?

2. **Observe Your Current Relationships:** Now, take a look at your current relationships. Write down any codependent behaviors you notice, such as people-pleasing, over-involvement, or fear of rejection.

3. **Acknowledge Patterns:** As you review your reflections, note any patterns that emerge. For instance, do you tend to feel responsible for others' emotions? Do you avoid expressing your own needs?

Recognizing these patterns can be eye-opening, and may feel uncomfortable at first. Remember, this exercise is about awareness, not self-judgment. Each behavior you identify is simply a starting point for growth.

Understanding Personal Triggers and Emotional Responses

Once you've started to identify your codependent behaviors, the next step is to understand what triggers these responses. Triggers are events, people, or situations that evoke strong emotional reactions, often rooted in past experiences. By recognizing your triggers, you can gain control over how you respond rather than allowing your emotions to dictate your actions.

Common Triggers in Codependency

Here are some common triggers for those with codependent tendencies. Take note if any of these resonate with your own experiences:

- **Fear of Conflict:** Avoiding confrontation or disagreement because it feels uncomfortable or makes you anxious.

- **Fear of Rejection:** Worrying that others will abandon or judge you if you express your needs or boundaries.

- **Feelings of Guilt:** Experiencing guilt when prioritizing yourself or saying "no," as if you are letting others down.

- **Uncertain Relationships:** Feeling uneasy or insecure in relationships where your role or value is unclear, leading to over-giving or people-pleasing to feel secure.

These triggers often stem from past experiences, such as early family dynamics, and may lead to heightened emotional responses. By becoming aware of your triggers, you can start to manage your reactions with greater control and self-compassion.

Exercise: Identifying and Managing Your Triggers

The following exercise will help you identify your personal triggers and develop strategies for managing your emotional responses.

1. **Observe Your Reactions:** For the next week, pay attention to moments when you feel strong emotional reactions. This might include feeling anxious, resentful, guilty, or unappreciated. Write down each experience, noting the specific trigger (such as a situation, comment, or behavior).

2. **Identify Patterns:** After a week, review your notes and look for recurring triggers. Are there specific situations or people that consistently evoke strong emotions? Recognize the themes that emerge, as these often point to unresolved

beliefs or fears.

3. **Develop Coping Strategies:** Once you've identified your triggers, brainstorm healthy ways to cope with these responses. For example:

- If conflict triggers fear, practice deep breathing or grounding exercises to calm yourself before responding.
- If saying "no" triggers guilt, remind yourself that setting boundaries is an act of self-respect and does not make you selfish.

This exercise helps you take ownership of your emotional responses, allowing you to respond thoughtfully rather than reactively. Over time, managing your triggers becomes easier, giving you greater control over your emotional world.

Cultivating a Healthy Sense of Self Separate from Relationships

One of the core challenges in codependency is developing a sense of self that isn't reliant on others' approval or validation. Many people with codependent tendencies find that their identity revolves around their roles in relationships—as caregivers, helpers, or peacekeepers. Cultivating a healthy sense of self means recognizing your intrinsic worth and understanding that you are valuable for who you are, not for what you do for others.

Building Self-Identity Beyond Relationships

To build a sense of self independent of relationships, it's essential to explore your own values, interests, and goals. This involves reconnecting with your inner desires and passions, separate from what others expect of you.

Exercise: Discovering Your Core Values and Interests

This exercise is designed to help you uncover the values, interests, and qualities that define you as an individual, apart from your relationships.

- **Identify Your Core Values:** Reflect on the qualities and principles that matter most to you. These might include honesty, creativity, kindness, independence, or compassion. Write down your top five values and think about how they influence your decisions and priorities.

- **Explore Your Interests:** Make a list of activities, hobbies, or topics that genuinely interest you. What are the things that make you feel happy, energized, or fulfilled? Remember, these don't have to be "productive" or impress anyone—they're simply for you.

- **Set Personal Goals:** Write down a few personal goals that reflect your values and interests. These goals could be as simple as taking a weekly art class, dedicating time to read each day, or starting a fitness routine. Focus on goals that bring you joy and satisfaction rather than those that please others.

As you engage in these self-reflective exercises, you'll begin to develop a clearer understanding of who you are beyond your relationships. This self-knowledge forms a strong foundation for making choices that honor your well-being, even when those choices differ from others' expectations.

Practicing Self-Validation

A healthy sense of self requires self-validation—the ability to acknowledge and affirm your own feelings, thoughts, and experiences.

When you rely solely on external validation, you may find yourself seeking approval, fearing disapproval, or changing your behavior to fit others' expectations. Self-validation, on the other hand, empowers you to trust yourself and make decisions that align with your values.

Exercise: Practicing Self-Validation

This exercise is designed to help you build a habit of validating your own thoughts and emotions rather than seeking constant external affirmation.

- **Recognize Your Emotions:** Throughout the day, take moments to check in with yourself and recognize your feelings without judgment. Acknowledge them as they are, even if they feel uncomfortable. For example, if you feel anxious, say to yourself, "I'm feeling anxious, and that's okay."

- **Affirm Your Experiences:** When you notice self-doubt or the urge to seek external validation, remind yourself of the validity of your feelings and experiences. Say something like, "My feelings are real and deserve respect," or "I trust myself to make the right choices for me."

- **Challenge Negative Self-Talk:** If you find yourself being overly critical, challenge these thoughts by reframing them with self-compassion. Replace "I'm not good enough" with "I'm doing my best, and that's enough."

Practicing self-validation reinforces your sense of self-worth and helps you recognize that you don't need external approval to feel whole. Over time, this practice becomes a valuable tool for maintaining emotional independence and building confidence.

Creating a Daily Practice of Self-Awareness

Building self-awareness is a continuous journey, and daily practices can help reinforce your progress. By setting aside time each day for reflection, you'll be able to stay connected to your inner self and cultivate habits that support your growth.

Exercise: Daily Self-Reflection Journal

A self-reflection journal is a powerful tool for deepening your self-awareness and tracking your progress over time.

1. **Set Aside Time Each Day:** Dedicate 5-10 minutes each evening to reflect on your day. Write down any thoughts, feelings, or observations that stand out. Focus on moments when you felt strong emotions or noticed codependent tendencies.

2. **Reflect on Personal Growth:** As you journal, note any progress you've made in recognizing patterns, managing triggers, or asserting your needs. Celebrate these small wins, as they represent meaningful steps toward change.

3. **Set Intentions for the Next Day:** At the end of each entry, set a simple intention for the following day. For example, "Tomorrow, I will practice self-validation," or "I will take five minutes to breathe if I feel overwhelmed."

This daily reflection practice helps you stay connected to your growth, reinforcing the changes you're making and empowering you to navigate each day with greater self-awareness.

Moving Forward

Cultivating self-awareness is a foundational part of healing from codependency. By recognizing your patterns, understanding your triggers, and developing a healthy sense of self, you're building the tools to live a life that honors your worth and respects your needs. Remember, this process is gradual, and each small step forward represents significant progress.

In the next chapter, we'll explore tools for emotional and cognitive healing, delving into practices that help you build resilience, address limiting beliefs, and strengthen your sense of self-worth. Together, these skills will support you in creating relationships and a life that reflect the true, authentic you.

Chapter 6

Emotional & Cognitive Healing

As you build self-awareness and recognize codependent patterns, the next step is to focus on emotional and cognitive healing. Codependency often leaves people with a negative self-concept, lingering shame, and unhelpful beliefs about their worth and relationships. This chapter introduces practical techniques for reshaping these internal narratives, managing stress and anxiety, and reframing limiting beliefs.

Healing emotionally and cognitively requires consistent practice and patience. It's about replacing negative self-talk with self-compassion, challenging thoughts that no longer serve you, and developing healthier, more empowering perspectives. By doing so, you can create a foundation of self-worth, resilience, and peace.

Addressing Negative Self-Concept and Shame

A negative self-concept, often rooted in shame, is one of the most common emotional burdens of codependency. People with codependent tendencies may carry deep feelings of inadequacy, believing that they're only worthy if they're helping or pleasing others. This shame-based self-view can lead to a harsh inner critic and persistent self-doubt.

Understanding the Source of Shame

Shame is different from guilt. Guilt is the feeling of remorse for something specific you've done, while shame is the feeling that there's something inherently wrong with who you are. This pervasive feeling often stems from early experiences where your worth or value was conditional, based on meeting others' needs or avoiding conflict. Understanding that shame was learned allows you to approach it with compassion, recognizing that it doesn't define your worth.

Exercise: Practicing Self-Compassion to Counter Shame

Self-compassion is a powerful antidote to shame. By treating yourself with kindness and understanding, you can start to release the weight of shame and develop a more positive self-concept.

- **Notice the Inner Critic:** The first step in practicing self-compassion is to become aware of your inner critic. Notice when you engage in negative self-talk or criticize yourself harshly. Write down these critical thoughts to identify patterns.

- **Challenge Negative Thoughts:** For each critical thought, write a compassionate response as if you were comforting a friend. For example, if you think, "I'm not good enough," reframe it with, "I'm doing my best, and that's enough."

- **Practice a Self-Compassionate Mantra:** Create a simple mantra that you can repeat during moments of shame or self-criticism. Examples include, "I am worthy of love and kindness," or "It's okay to be imperfect; I am enough as

I am." Repeat this mantra daily or whenever you need to counter negative self-talk.

Practicing self-compassion won't erase shame overnight. However, it creates a safe inner environment where you can gradually let go of self-criticism and begin to value yourself for who you are, not just what you do for others.

Tools for Managing Stress, Anxiety, and Obsessive Thoughts

People struggling with codependency often experience high levels of stress and anxiety, particularly around relationships. These feelings can create a cycle of worry, obsessive thoughts, and emotional exhaustion. Learning to manage these emotions is crucial for emotional healing and self-care.

Understanding Anxiety and Obsessive Thoughts

Anxiety is a natural response to uncertainty or perceived threats, and it often manifests as a series of "what if" questions or worst-case scenarios. Obsessive thoughts, which can accompany anxiety, are repetitive, unwanted thoughts that keep you stuck in a loop of worry. For those with codependent tendencies, anxiety often revolves around fears of rejection, conflict, or losing control in relationships.

Grounding Techniques for Stress and Anxiety

Grounding exercises are simple, effective tools that bring your focus back to the present moment, helping to reduce anxiety and calm obsessive thoughts. Here are a few grounding techniques to try:

1. **The 5-4-3-2-1 Technique:** This technique engages your senses to ground you in the present.
   - Look around and identify 5 things you can see.

- Identify 4 things you can touch.
- Identify 3 things you can hear.
- Identify 2 things you can smell.
- Identify 1 thing you can taste.

This exercise shifts your focus away from anxious thoughts and brings you back to the present.

2. **Deep Breathing:** Deep, slow breaths activate the body's relaxation response, calming anxiety. Try the "4-7-8" breathing technique:

- Breathe in deeply for 4 counts.
- Hold your breath for 7 counts.
- Exhale slowly for 8 counts.
- Repeat this several times, focusing on the sensation of your breath.

3. **Visualization:** Imagine a safe, peaceful place in your mind, like a beach or a forest. Close your eyes and focus on the sights, sounds, and sensations of this place. This visualization can help you feel grounded and calm.

These techniques help manage stress in the moment, allowing you to regain control over anxious or obsessive thoughts.

Practicing Cognitive Restructuring to Challenge Anxiety

Cognitive restructuring is a technique that helps you challenge and reframe anxious thoughts, replacing them with more balanced perspectives.

1. **Identify the Anxious Thought:** Write down the specific thought causing you anxiety. For example, "If I don't help, they'll be upset with me."

2. **Challenge the Thought:** Ask yourself, "Is this thought based on facts or assumptions?" or "What evidence sup-

ports or contradicts this thought?"

3. **Reframe the Thought:** Replace the anxious thought with a balanced one, such as, "I am allowed to set boundaries, and others' reactions are their responsibility."

Practicing cognitive restructuring regularly can reduce anxiety and obsessive thinking, empowering you to make decisions based on your well-being rather than fear.

Reframing Limiting Beliefs About Self-Worth and Relationships

Limiting beliefs are deeply held assumptions about yourself, others, or the world that restrict your potential and hinder your growth. For many people with codependent tendencies, limiting beliefs revolve around self-worth, relationships, and control. These beliefs may sound like "I'm only lovable if I help others" or "Setting boundaries will push people away." Reframing these beliefs is key to emotional healing, as it allows you to approach life with a more empowering, self-supportive mindset.

Common Limiting Beliefs in Codependency

Here are some common limiting beliefs that often arise in codependency. See if any of these resonate with you:

- "I am only valuable if others need me." This belief ties self-worth to being helpful or indispensable, creating a sense of dependency on others for validation.
- "If I prioritize myself, I am selfish." This belief leads to self-neglect, as you may feel guilty or "wrong" for setting boundaries or focusing on your needs.
- "Conflict means the end of a relationship." This belief can create an intense fear of conflict, causing you to avoid asserting

yourself to maintain peace.

• "I must control others to feel safe." This belief can lead to over-involvement in others' lives, as you may feel responsible for ensuring they're happy or secure.

These beliefs often stem from early experiences or societal messages, but they can be changed with practice and intentional reframing.

Exercise: Reframing Limiting Beliefs

The following exercise will guide you in identifying and reframing limiting beliefs, helping you adopt a more supportive and empowering mindset.

1. **Identify a Limiting Belief:** Choose one limiting belief that you notice frequently. For example, "I am only valuable if others need me."

2. **Examine the Origin:** Reflect on where this belief might have come from. Did it originate in childhood, a specific relationship, or a cultural message? Understanding the origin can help you see that this belief was learned, not inherent.

3. **Challenge the Belief:** Question the belief by asking, "Is this belief always true?" or "What evidence contradicts this belief?" Recognize instances where you've been valuable or worthy outside of this belief.

4. **Reframe the Belief:** Replace the limiting belief with a supportive one. For example, you might reframe "I am only valuable if others need me" to "I am valuable for who I am, not just what I do for others."

5. **Practice Affirmations:** Write down your reframed belief and turn it into a positive affirmation, such as, "I am inherently valuable and worthy of love." Repeat this affirmation

daily to reinforce the new belief.

Reframing limiting beliefs is a gradual process, but each time you challenge a negative belief, you strengthen your sense of self-worth and build resilience against codependent patterns.

Building a Routine for Emotional and Cognitive Healing

Healing from codependency involves creating routines that support emotional regulation, self-worth, and mental clarity. By incorporating these practices into your daily life, you start to build a foundation for long-term growth and well-being.

Morning Intentions for Emotional Resilience

Starting your day with intention can set a positive tone for how you approach challenges and relationships.

1. **Set a Daily Intention:** Each morning, set a simple intention that reflects a positive change you want to make. Examples include, "Today, I will honor my boundaries," or "I will show myself kindness."

2. **Practice a Grounding Exercise:** Begin your day with a grounding exercise, like deep breathing or visualization, to center yourself and reduce anxiety.

3. **Affirm Self-Worth:** Recite an affirmation that reinforces your inherent value, such as, "I am worthy of love and respect, just as I am."

By starting your day with intention, grounding, and self-affirmation, you equip yourself to handle whatever challenges arise with resilience and self-compassion.

Evening Reflection for Self-Growth

Ending your day with reflection allows you to process emotions, release stress, and acknowledge your growth.

1. **Journal Your Emotions:** Write down any strong emotions or thoughts you experienced during the day. Reflect on how you managed your reactions and note any progress you made in handling triggers.

2. **Celebrate Small Wins:** Acknowledge any positive steps you took, such as setting a boundary, reframing a belief, or practicing self-compassion. These small wins build momentum and reinforce your progress.

3. **Set a Positive Intention for Tomorrow:** End your reflection by setting an intention for the next day. This can be something simple, like, "Tomorrow, I will listen to my needs," or "I will approach challenges with patience."

These routines support emotional and cognitive healing by reinforcing healthy habits and fostering a compassionate relationship with yourself.

Moving Forward

Emotional and cognitive healing are essential parts of breaking free from codependency. By addressing shame, managing anxiety, and reframing limiting beliefs, you're building the skills to navigate life with resilience and self-respect. This process takes time, but each exercise and practice contributes to a stronger sense of self-worth and inner peace.

In the next chapter, we'll dive into the importance of setting and maintaining boundaries, a critical skill for protecting your well-being and fostering healthy, balanced relationships. Each step you take is

bringing you closer to a life of freedom, self-empowerment, and
genuine connection.

Chapter 7

Setting & Maintaining Boundaries

ONE OF THE MOST TRANSFORMATIVE SKILLS in healing from codependency is the ability to set and maintain healthy boundaries. Boundaries are essential for creating balanced relationships, protecting your well-being, and fostering a sense of self-respect. Without boundaries, you may find yourself feeling overwhelmed, undervalued, or even resentful as you put others' needs ahead of your own. Learning to set boundaries is about honoring your needs and creating mutually respectful and supportive relationships.

In this chapter, we'll explore what healthy boundaries look like, provide steps for establishing boundaries across different types of relationships, and discuss how to handle pushback or resistance when others challenge your limits. By the end, you'll have the tools to approach boundaries with confidence, ensuring that your relationships support, rather than diminish, your well-being.

Understanding Healthy Boundaries

Boundaries are the limits and guidelines we establish to protect our physical, emotional, and mental well-being. Healthy boundaries communicate what is acceptable and unacceptable, helping you maintain a sense of autonomy in your relationships. Boundaries aren't about pushing people away; instead, they're about creating a structure where both parties' needs are respected.

Key Aspects of Healthy Boundaries

Healthy boundaries are characterized by clarity, respect, and flexibility. Here are some qualities of healthy boundaries:

- **Clarity:** Healthy boundaries are specific and clearly communicated. When you set a boundary, you let others know exactly what you're comfortable with and what you're not.

- **Mutual Respect:** Healthy boundaries respect both your needs and those of others. They're not about controlling others but rather about ensuring mutual respect in interactions.

- **Flexibility:** Boundaries can evolve as relationships grow or as situations change. Flexibility allows you to adjust your boundaries to reflect your current needs and priorities.

- **Emotional Protection:** Healthy boundaries protect your emotional well-being by preventing over-giving, resentment, or burnout. They ensure that you don't sacrifice your own needs to please or accommodate others.

Setting boundaries may feel challenging at first, especially if you've been accustomed to codependent dynamics. Remember, boundaries are not selfish; they're acts of self-respect that allow you to engage in relationships with integrity and confidence.

Steps for Establishing Boundaries in Different Types of Relationships

Boundaries can vary depending on the nature of the relationship. Below are guidelines for setting boundaries in family, friendships, romantic, and professional relationships.

1. Family Relationships

Family relationships can be some of the most challenging when it comes to boundaries, as family dynamics are often deeply rooted and emotionally charged. Setting boundaries with family may feel difficult, especially if you fear conflict or judgment. However, healthy boundaries are essential for creating a sense of autonomy within your family.

Steps for Setting Boundaries with Family:

1. **Identify Your Limits:** Reflect on situations with family members that make you feel uncomfortable, disrespected, or overwhelmed. Examples might include unsolicited advice, questions about your personal life, or expectations to spend time together.

2. **Communicate Clearly and Calmly:** When setting a boundary with family, be direct and specific. For example, "I appreciate your concern, but I'd prefer to handle this decision on my own," or "I need some quiet time after work, so I'll join family gatherings a bit later in the evening."

3. **Stick to Your Boundaries:** Family members may push back, especially if they're used to certain dynamics. Be prepared to repeat your boundary if necessary, calmly reinforcing your position.

4. **Offer Alternatives When Possible:** If a family member feels disappointed by your boundary, consider offering alternatives that work for you. For example, if you're setting a boundary around visiting frequency, suggest specific times that feel manageable.

Setting boundaries with family takes practice and patience, but it's a critical step toward developing a healthy, respectful relationship with your loved ones.

2. Friendships

Friendships are often based on mutual support and understanding, but they can still benefit from clear boundaries. Sometimes, friendships may involve blurred boundaries, where one person feels responsible for solving the other's problems or is expected to be constantly available.

Steps for Setting Boundaries in Friendships:

1. **Clarify Your Availability:** If a friend frequently reaches out for support at inconvenient times, communicate your availability clearly. For example, "I'd love to talk, but I have a busy schedule during the week. Can we plan a time to catch up?"

2. **Express Your Limits on Emotional Support:** While friends support each other, it's essential to avoid taking on a friend's burdens as your own. If a friend often vents about the same issue without seeking solutions, you might say, "I care about you and want to help, but I feel that listening alone isn't enough. Have you considered other resources that could support you?"

3. **Create Boundaries Around Shared Activities:** If your friend invites you to activities that you're not interested in or that conflict with your needs, feel free to decline. You could say, "I'm not really interested in this activity, but I'd love to join you for something else."

Boundaries in friendships foster mutual respect and prevent one-sided dynamics, ensuring that your friendships are a source of support rather than stress.

3. Romantic Relationships

Boundaries in romantic relationships are essential for creating a sense of individuality within the partnership. It can be easy to fall into patterns of over-reliance, but boundaries allow both partners to thrive independently while staying connected.

Steps for Setting Boundaries in Romantic Relationships:

1. **Define Your Personal Space:** Communicate your needs for alone time, even within a close relationship. For example, "I love spending time with you, but I also need some personal time to recharge."

2. **Set Boundaries Around Communication:** If you feel overwhelmed by constant texting or calls, set a communication boundary. For example, "I'd prefer to have some focused time during the day and catch up in the evenings."

3. **Address Financial Boundaries:** If finances are shared, it's important to agree on spending limits, shared expenses, and individual contributions. Setting clear financial boundaries can prevent misunderstandings and tension.

4. **Express Emotional Needs and Limits:** It's natural to lean on each other in a relationship, but it's important to

communicate when you need space to process your emotions or if certain topics feel overwhelming.

Clear boundaries in romantic relationships allow both partners to feel secure, supported, and respected, helping to create a balanced and fulfilling relationship.

4. Professional Relationships

Setting boundaries in your work life is crucial for maintaining a healthy work-life balance and protecting your mental and emotional well-being. Professional boundaries help prevent burnout and ensure that your responsibilities remain manageable.

Steps for Setting Boundaries in Professional Relationships:

1. **Set Limits on Availability:** If you're frequently contacted outside of work hours, communicate your availability. For example, "I'm available from 9 AM to 5 PM; I'll respond to emails or messages during those hours."

2. **Establish Boundaries Around Responsibilities:** If you find yourself taking on tasks outside your job description, it's okay to say no. Try, "I'd love to help, but my current workload doesn't allow for additional projects."

3. **Address Personal Boundaries:** In some workplaces, it's common for colleagues to ask personal questions. If you're uncomfortable sharing personal details, redirect the conversation politely by saying, "I prefer to keep my personal life private."

4. **Communicate Your Needs for Focus Time:** If colleagues frequently interrupt you, set boundaries around focus time. For example, "I'm dedicating this hour to focused work, but I'll be available afterward if you need me."

Professional boundaries help you maintain control over your work environment, allowing you to perform at your best without sacrificing your personal well-being.

How to Handle Pushback and Maintain Boundaries in the Face of Resistance

When you set boundaries, especially with people who are accustomed to particular dynamics, it's not uncommon to face resistance or pushback. Some may react with frustration, guilt-tripping, or attempts to dismiss your needs. Standing firm in the face of resistance is essential for maintaining your well-being and reinforcing the value of your boundaries.

Common Forms of Pushback

Here are some common ways people may resist boundaries, along with strategies for handling them:

1. **Guilt-Tripping:** Some may try to make you feel guilty for setting boundaries, suggesting that you're "selfish" or "uncaring."

- **How to Respond:** Remind yourself that setting boundaries is an act of self-respect, not selfishness. You might say, "I understand that this may feel disappointing, but I need to honor my limits to stay balanced."

2. **Dismissal:** Others may dismiss your boundary, saying things like "You're being too sensitive" or "It's not that big of a deal."

- **How to Respond:** Reinforce your boundary calmly and assertively, without over-explaining. Try, "This is important to me, and I need you to respect it."

3. **Anger or Hostility:** Some may react with anger, especially if they're accustomed to getting their way. They may become defensive or lash out.

- **How to Respond:** Stay calm and avoid engaging in an argument. You can say, "I understand this may be difficult to hear, but I need this boundary for my well-being."

4. **Repeated Attempts to Violate the Boundary:** Some people may test your boundary, continuing to behave as if it doesn't exist.

- **How to Respond:** Be consistent and firm. Each time they cross the line, restate the boundary without yielding. Consistency reinforces the boundary and shows that you're serious.

By anticipating and preparing for pushback, you empower yourself to handle resistance confidently. If you remain consistent, others will likely come to respect your boundaries over time.

The Benefits of Boundaries for Personal Growth and Relationship Health

Setting and maintaining boundaries isn't just about protecting yourself from discomfort or intrusion; it's a key component of personal growth and healthy relationships. Some of the benefits of boundaries are:

- **Increased Self-Respect:** Boundaries reinforce your sense of self-worth, showing that you value your well-being.
- **Enhanced Relationships:** Healthy boundaries create clear expectations, reduce resentment, and foster mutual respect.
- **Reduced Stress and Anxiety:** Boundaries help prevent burnout by ensuring that your energy and resources aren't overextended.

- **Greater Independence:** By setting boundaries, you allow yourself to thrive as an individual, free from the pressures of people-pleasing or over-giving.

Each boundary you set is a statement of self-care and respect, supporting a life where your needs and well-being are prioritized.

Moving Forward

Learning to set and maintain boundaries is a transformative skill that can lead to more fulfilling relationships and a stronger sense of self-worth. While it may feel challenging at first, each boundary you set reinforces your right to prioritize your own well-being and live authentically. Remember, boundaries are not about rejection; they're about respect—both for yourself and for others.

In the next chapter, we'll explore the importance of developing emotional independence. This skill further enhances your sense of self and allows you to navigate relationships with confidence and resilience. By building emotional independence, you'll find greater freedom and fulfillment in relationships, empowered by a foundation of inner strength and self-respect.

PART III

Chapter 8

Healing the Inner Child

AS YOU MOVE FORWARD ON YOUR JOURNEY to overcome codependency and establish healthier relationships, it's important to recognize and connect with a part of yourself that may hold some of your deepest wounds: your inner child. The "inner child" represents the younger, vulnerable version of yourself that still carries the emotional impact of early experiences. When these experiences involve neglect, criticism, or unmet needs, the inner child can become wounded, holding on to fears, insecurities, and beliefs that continue to affect your adult life.

Healing the inner child is a process of reconnecting with this part of yourself, acknowledging past wounds, and providing the love, compassion, and support you may not have received during childhood. This chapter will guide you through exercises to connect with your inner child, acknowledge past wounds, and build a compassionate relationship with yourself. By healing your inner child, you'll develop a stronger foundation of self-worth, inner peace, and resilience, empowering you to live more authentically and free from old emotional patterns.

Understanding the Inner Child

The concept of the inner child is nestled in the idea that we all carry a younger version of ourselves within us, along with the feelings, needs, and vulnerabilities we experienced as children. This part of ourselves doesn't disappear as we age; instead, it exists as an emotional memory that can influence our thoughts, behaviors, and relationships.

For many people with codependent tendencies, the inner child may have learned to feel responsible for others' emotions, to prioritize others' needs over their own, or to fear abandonment. These patterns often arise in response to early experiences of neglect, emotional invalidation, or inconsistent caregiving. Healing the inner child involves acknowledging these wounds and providing the validation, love, and understanding that may have been missing.

Signs That Your Inner Child Needs Healing

Here are some signs that your inner child may be carrying unhealed wounds:

- **Fear of Abandonment:** A deep-seated fear of being left alone or rejected, often leading to clinginess, people-pleasing, or difficulty setting boundaries.
- **Low Self-Worth:** Feelings of inadequacy or self-doubt, as if you're "not good enough" or only valuable when helping others.
- **Difficulty Trusting Others:** Challenges in trusting people or forming close connections, stemming from past experiences of betrayal or inconsistency.
- **Emotional Reactivity:** Intense emotional responses to seemingly minor events, often linked to unresolved childhood wounds.

- **Self-Criticism and Perfectionism:** A harsh inner critic that tells you to be "perfect" to avoid judgment or disapproval, often reflecting past criticism from your caregivers.

Recognizing these patterns can be a valuable step toward understanding how your inner child may be affecting your present life. These behaviors are not flaws—they are coping mechanisms that helped you survive difficult situations in childhood. Now, as an adult, you have the power to help your inner child heal and to provide the support they've always needed.

Exercises to Connect with Your Inner Child

Connecting with your inner child allows you to recognize and honor the part of you that carries your earliest emotional experiences. This process may feel unfamiliar or even uncomfortable at first, but it's a compassionate way to address past wounds and create a nurturing relationship with yourself.

Exercise 1: Visualize Your Inner Child

Visualization is a powerful tool for connecting with your inner child. This exercise allows you to form a mental image of your younger self, creating a safe space for healing.

1. **Find a Quiet Place:** Sit comfortably in a quiet space where you won't be disturbed. Close your eyes and take a few deep breaths, allowing yourself to relax.

2. **Picture Your Younger Self:** Visualize yourself as a child. This could be at any age that feels significant, whether it's a happy memory or a time when you felt vulnerable. Imagine what you looked like, the clothes you wore, and your expression.

3. **Observe with Compassion:** Imagine yourself approach-

ing your inner child with kindness. Notice how your inner child feels—are they sad, lonely, scared, or perhaps in need of comfort? Simply observe without judgment.

4. **Offer Reassurance:** Gently tell your inner child, "I'm here for you. I see you, and I love you just as you are." Offer words of reassurance, letting them know they are safe and valued.

5. **Hold Space for Emotions:** If any emotions come up during this exercise, allow yourself to feel them fully. This may include sadness, grief, or even joy. Embrace these feelings as part of your healing process.

Connecting with your inner child through visualization is a simple way to begin the healing process. Repeat this exercise whenever you feel disconnected or in need of emotional support.

Exercise 2: Write a Letter to Your Inner Child

Writing a letter to your inner child is a powerful way to express compassion, validate their experiences, and acknowledge the pain they may have carried for years.

1. **Begin with Empathy:** Start your letter by acknowledging your inner child's feelings and experiences. For example, "Dear [Your Name as a Child], I know you felt lonely, scared, or unworthy at times, and I'm sorry you went through that."

2. **Validate Their Feelings:** Validate any emotions that come up, letting your inner child know it was okay to feel hurt, confused, or scared. Write from a place of understanding and compassion, affirming that their feelings were real and valid.

3. **Offer Reassurance:** Assure your inner child that they are

loved, valued, and enough, regardless of what others may have said or done. Remind them that they don't have to be "perfect" to be worthy of love.

4. **Express Support:** Conclude your letter by letting your inner child know that you are here for them now. Tell them, "I will protect and care for you. I'm here to help you feel safe and loved."

Writing a letter to your inner child can be a profoundly emotional experience, as it allows you to confront past wounds and offer the love and compassion you may not have received. Save this letter as a reminder of the relationship you're building with yourself.

Acknowledging Past Wounds and Unmet Needs

Healing your inner child involves acknowledging the wounds you experienced in the past and recognizing the needs that went unmet. This process is not about blaming or dwelling on the past; instead, it's about understanding how these experiences shaped you and creating space for healing.

Exercise: Reflect on Past Wounds and Unmet Needs

This exercise encourages you to reflect on your early experiences and identify any emotional wounds or needs that may still impact you today.

1. **Identify Key Childhood Experiences:** Reflect on any childhood memories that stand out as particularly painful or impactful. These could include experiences of neglect, criticism, lack of affection, or feeling unsupported.

2. **Recognize Unmet Needs:** For each memory, consider what you needed at the time. Perhaps you needed reassurance, understanding, or a sense of safety. Write down these

needs, acknowledging that they were valid and important.

3. **Forgive Yourself:** If you feel guilt or shame about how these wounds have affected you, practice self-forgiveness. Remind yourself that these experiences were beyond your control and that you did the best you could with the resources you had.

Acknowledging past wounds and unmet needs helps you develop empathy for your inner child. By recognizing these experiences, you empower yourself to begin meeting these needs in the present, building a healthier and more compassionate relationship with yourself.

Building Compassion and Trust Within Yourself

One of the most powerful ways to heal your inner child is by cultivating self-compassion and trust. Self-compassion allows you to approach yourself with kindness rather than criticism and helps you create an inner environment where you feel safe, valued, and understood. Building trust within yourself strengthens your sense of inner stability, giving your inner child the security they may not have had in the past.

Practicing Self-Compassion

Self-compassion involves treating yourself with the same kindness, patience, and understanding that you would offer a friend. When your inner child feels seen and understood, it can help alleviate feelings of shame or unworthiness.

Exercise: Self-Compassionate Self-Talk:

1. **Notice Self-Critical Thoughts:** When you catch yourself engaging in self-criticism, pause and recognize that these

thoughts often stem from past wounds.

2. **Replace Criticism with Kindness:** Replace self-critical thoughts with compassionate statements. For example, if you think, "I should have done better," reframe it with, "I did the best I could with what I knew at the time."

3. **Reassure Your Inner Child:** Speak to your inner child with gentle, supportive words. Tell them, "It's okay to make mistakes. You are loved and worthy, just as you are."

Practicing self-compassion regularly reinforces the message that you are deserving of love and kindness, creating a nurturing relationship with your inner child.

Building Self-Trust

Trusting yourself is a crucial part of inner child healing, as it provides a sense of security and stability. Self-trust means honoring your feelings, listening to your needs, and believing in your ability to make choices that serve your well-being.

Exercise: Honoring Your Inner Child's Needs:

1. **Listen to Your Emotions:** Emotions often signal underlying needs. When you feel sadness, anger, or anxiety, take a moment to ask yourself what you need in that moment. It might be rest, reassurance, or connection.

2. **Act on Your Needs:** Whenever possible, respond to your needs in a way that respects and honors them. For example, if you need a break, give yourself permission to rest without guilt.

3. **Acknowledge Your Progress:** Building self-trust is a gradual process. Each time you listen to and honor your needs, take a moment to acknowledge your progress. Remind

yourself that you are learning to care for yourself in a new, empowering way.

Building self-trust allows you to create an inner relationship that is rooted in respect and compassion, helping your inner child feel safe and valued.

Integrating Inner Child Healing into Daily Life

Healing the inner child is an ongoing journey that involves making small, consistent choices to care for and nurture this vulnerable part of yourself. Integrating these practices into your daily life can help you maintain a strong connection with your inner child, reinforcing your self-worth and resilience.

Daily Affirmations for Your Inner Child

Affirmations are positive statements that reinforce self-worth, compassion, and love. Practicing affirmations regularly can help soothe your inner child and build a positive self-image.

Examples of Daily Affirmations:

- "I am safe, loved, and worthy, just as I am."
- "I trust myself to make choices that honor my well-being."
- "I am kind to myself, and I deserve compassion and respect."
- "My past does not define my worth. I am whole and complete."

Choose an affirmation that resonates with you and repeat it daily, either in the morning or whenever you need reassurance. These affirmations help create an inner environment that is nurturing and supportive.

Engaging in Activities That Bring Joy

Engaging in joyful activities that connect you to your inner child can be deeply healing. Think back to the activities you loved as a child, such as drawing, playing outdoors, or listening to music, and make time for them in your routine. Allow yourself to engage in these activities without judgment, simply for the joy they bring.

Connecting with your inner child in this way allows you to experience pure enjoyment and playfulness, fostering a deeper sense of self-compassion and freedom.

Moving Forward with Inner Child Healing

Healing your inner child is a journey that requires patience, compassion, and consistency. Each time you connect with your inner child, you reinforce a sense of self-worth, resilience, and inner peace. By acknowledging past wounds, validating unmet needs, and providing love and compassion, you offer your inner child the healing they've longed for.

In the next chapter, we'll explore the concept of emotional independence, building on the inner foundation of self-compassion and trust you've cultivated. Emotional independence allows you to engage in relationships from a place of strength and authenticity, free from the need for validation or approval. Each step forward brings you closer to a life where your worth, happiness, and fulfillment come from within, empowering you to live fully and authentically.

Chapter 9

Developing Emotional Independence

ONE OF THE MOST EMPOWERING STEPS in overcoming codependency is developing emotional independence. Emotional independence means being able to manage your emotions, find inner stability, and fulfill your own needs without relying on others for constant validation or support. For those accustomed to people-pleasing and prioritizing others, developing emotional independence can be transformative, allowing you to experience relationships from a place of confidence, balance, and self-respect.

In this chapter, we'll explore practical strategies to stop people-pleasing and prioritize your own needs, techniques for emotional detachment that allow you to maintain relationships without losing yourself, and self-soothing methods to build inner resilience. By cultivating emotional independence, you'll learn to navigate relationships with authenticity and strength, freeing yourself from dependency and building a life that genuinely reflects your values and desires.

How to Stop People-Pleasing and Prioritize Personal Needs

People-pleasing is a common pattern in codependency, often fueled by a fear of rejection, conflict, or disapproval. Many people-pleasers believe their worth is tied to how well they serve others, making it difficult to prioritize their own needs. While kindness and generosity are positive qualities, people-pleasing becomes problematic when it leads to self-neglect and resentment.

Recognizing the Root of People-Pleasing

People-pleasing often stems from early experiences where love or approval was conditional, based on how well you met others' expectations. Over time, this behavior can become a way to avoid conflict and ensure connection, even if it comes at the expense of your well-being.

Common signs of people-pleasing include:

- Difficulty Saying No: Agreeing to requests or favors, even when it's inconvenient or against your own interests.
- Fear of Disappointing Others: Worrying that asserting your needs will lead to rejection, criticism, or conflict.
- Seeking Approval: Constantly looking for reassurance or validation from others, often feeling anxious without it.
- Prioritizing Others' Needs: Putting others' happiness before your own, even if it leaves you feeling drained or unfulfilled.

Recognizing these patterns is the first step in breaking free from people-pleasing. From here, you can begin to prioritize your own needs without guilt or fear.

Exercise: Practicing Saying "No" with Confidence

Learning to say "no" can be challenging, especially if you're used to putting others first. This exercise will help you practice assertive refusal while respecting both your needs and the other person's feelings.

1. Start Small: Begin with minor requests or situations where saying "no" feels manageable. For example, if a friend asks for a small favor that you'd rather decline, use this opportunity to practice.

2. Use Assertive Language: Practice saying "no" in a way that is clear, kind, and respectful. For example, "I appreciate you asking, but I'm unable to help with that right now."

3. Hold Your Ground: People may try to negotiate or persuade you to change your answer. Stay firm in your response, politely repeating, "I'm sorry, but I can't help this time."

4. Reflect on Your Feelings: Afterward, reflect on how it felt to say "no." Acknowledge any guilt or discomfort, but also celebrate the progress you made in prioritizing your needs.

Over time, practicing saying "no" builds confidence, reinforcing the message that your needs are just as important as others'. This helps you establish a healthy balance, allowing you to give from a place of fullness rather than obligation.

Techniques for Emotional Detachment Without Isolation

Emotional detachment doesn't mean cutting yourself off from others or becoming unfeeling; rather, it's about creating a healthy sense of separation that allows you to engage in relationships without losing yourself. Emotional detachment involves managing your emotions and remaining calm, even when others are struggling or behaving in ways that might have previously triggered a reaction.

What is Healthy Emotional Detachment?

Healthy emotional detachment allows you to support others without absorbing their emotions or feeling responsible for their happiness. This skill is particularly helpful for those with codependent tendencies, as it prevents over-involvement and emotional burnout.

Benefits of healthy detachment include:

- **Reduced Anxiety:** Detachment allows you to remain grounded, even in emotionally charged situations, reducing anxiety and emotional overwhelm.

- **Enhanced Self-Control:** By not reacting impulsively to others' emotions or behaviors, you gain more control over your own responses.

- **Increased Compassion:** Detachment actually allows you to show more empathy and compassion, as you're able to support others without becoming consumed by their emotions.

Exercise: Practicing Emotional Detachment

This exercise will help you practice emotional detachment in a way that maintains empathy and compassion without over-involvement.

1. **Observe Your Emotions:** When you notice yourself becoming emotionally entangled in someone else's situation, pause and take a few deep breaths. Observe your own emotions and remind yourself that these feelings belong to you, not the other person.

2. **Create Mental Boundaries:** Visualize an invisible boundary between you and the other person. Imagine that their emotions, opinions, or needs exist on the other side of this boundary while you remain grounded in your own feelings.

3. **Focus on Compassionate Support:** Shift your focus from "fixing" or "absorbing" their feelings to simply offering

compassion. Say to yourself, "I can empathize without taking on their emotions. Their happiness is their responsibility."

4. **Practice Detachment Phrases:** Use self-talk to reinforce detachment, such as, "I am here for support, but I am not responsible for their choices or feelings."

By practicing emotional detachment, you empower yourself to engage in relationships with balance and resilience, allowing others to take responsibility for their own emotions and well-being.

Self-Soothing Methods and Resilience-Building Practices

Self-soothing is an essential skill for managing stress and regulating emotions, especially when you're accustomed to relying on others for comfort or reassurance. By developing the ability to soothe yourself, you build resilience and cultivate inner peace, allowing you to handle challenges with greater confidence.

Self-Soothing Techniques

Self-soothing involves using calming strategies to comfort yourself in moments of distress, anxiety, or sadness. Here are a few effective self-soothing techniques:

1. **Deep Breathing:** Deep breathing activates the body's relaxation response, reducing stress and promoting calm. Try the 4-7-8 breathing technique:

   - Inhale for 4 counts, hold for 7 counts, and exhale for 8 counts.
   - Repeat this cycle 3-5 times to calm your nervous system.

2. **Progressive Muscle Relaxation (PMR):** PMR involves tensing and relaxing each muscle group to release physical tension and create a sense of relaxation.

- Start by tensing your feet and holding for 5 seconds, then release.
- Gradually work your way up through each muscle group, from legs to shoulders, until you've relaxed your entire body.
3. **Visualization:** Visualize a peaceful, comforting place where you feel safe and relaxed, such as a beach or forest. Focus on the sights, sounds, and sensations of this place, allowing your mind to escape from stress.
4. **Self-Compassionate Touch:** Physical touch can be grounding and comforting. Place a hand over your heart or gently hold your own hand, offering yourself words of reassurance, such as, "I'm here for you. You're safe, and you'll get through this."

These self-soothing techniques can be practiced daily or whenever you feel overwhelmed, helping you cultivate an internal source of comfort and stability.

Building Emotional Resilience

Emotional resilience is the ability to adapt and recover from stress, adversity, and challenges. It allows you to handle setbacks more easily and empowers you to face life's difficulties without becoming overwhelmed. Building resilience is especially helpful for those working to break free from codependent patterns, as it strengthens inner stability and promotes independence.

Exercises to Build Emotional Resilience

Here are some exercises to help you build resilience over time:
1. **Practice Positive Reframing:** Positive reframing involves shifting your perspective to find constructive ways of viewing difficult situations. For example:

- Instead of thinking, "I failed," reframe it as "This experience taught me something valuable."

- Positive reframing doesn't mean ignoring challenges but instead finding lessons or opportunities for growth.

2. **Set Small, Achievable Goals:** Building resilience requires a sense of accomplishment and self-efficacy. Set small, realistic goals each day that help you feel productive and capable. Each accomplishment, no matter how minor, reinforces your confidence and resilience.

3. **Cultivate a Support Network:** Healthy social connections often bolster emotional resilience. Surround yourself with people who support your growth, respect your boundaries, and encourage your independence. Lean on these connections for encouragement, but remain mindful of maintaining balance and reciprocity.

4. **Accept and Normalize Discomfort:** Resilience involves learning to tolerate discomfort, recognizing that difficult emotions are a part of life. When you face challenges, remind yourself that it's okay to feel uncomfortable and that these feelings will pass. Approach discomfort with curiosity, asking, "What can I learn from this experience?"

Each of these practices strengthens your ability to handle adversity, empowering you to face challenges from a place of confidence and self-trust.

Integrating Emotional Independence into Daily Life

Building emotional independence is an ongoing process, but integrating these practices into your daily life can reinforce your sense of inner stability and confidence. Here are some ways to practice emotional independence on a daily basis:

1. Start Your Day with a Self-Check-In

Each morning, take a few moments to check in with yourself. Notice how you feel emotionally and mentally, and ask yourself what you need that day. Setting a daily intention, such as "Today, I will prioritize my well-being" or "I will trust myself to make decisions that serve me," reinforces your commitment to emotional independence.

2. Practice Daily Self-Validation

Throughout the day, practice validating your own thoughts and feelings. Rather than seeking reassurance from others, remind yourself that your emotions are valid. If you're feeling uncertain, tell yourself, "It's okay to feel this way," or "I trust myself to make the best choice for me."

3. Journal to Reflect and Process Emotions

Journaling is a powerful tool for self-reflection and emotional processing. Set aside a few minutes each evening to write about your day, noting any situations that triggered strong emotions or people-pleasing tendencies. Reflect on how you handled these situations and celebrate any progress you made in asserting yourself or maintaining boundaries.

4. Embrace Solitude as an Act of Self-Care

Emotional independence often involves finding comfort in solitude. Embrace moments of solitude as an opportunity to recharge and reconnect with yourself. Use this time to engage in activities that bring you joy, relaxation, or fulfillment, whether it's reading, painting, exercising, or simply enjoying a quiet moment.

Moving Forward

Developing emotional independence is a vital step toward building a life rooted in self-worth, resilience, and inner peace. By learning to stop people-pleasing, practicing emotional detachment, and cultivating self-soothing techniques, you're creating a foundation of strength and stability that empowers you to engage in relationships from a place of confidence and balance.

In the next chapter, we'll explore reclaiming your sense of identity and autonomy, building on the foundation of emotional independence you've cultivated. You'll learn strategies to reconnect with your passions, pursue personal goals, and create a life that reflects your authentic self. Each step forward brings you closer to a life of fulfillment, freedom, and genuine self-worth.

Chapter 10

Reclaiming Your Identity & Autonomy

As you journey toward healing and self-discovery, one of the most powerful steps you can take is reclaiming your identity and autonomy. Codependency often involves a pattern of losing yourself in others' needs, expectations, or demands, which can erode your sense of who you are. Reclaiming your identity and autonomy is about reconnecting with your values, desires, and dreams, allowing you to build a life that reflects your authentic self.

In this chapter, we'll explore activities to rediscover your personal interests, goals, and values and craft a life plan that aligns with who you truly are. We'll also work on strengthening your self-esteem and autonomy, empowering you to navigate life with confidence, independence, and purpose. By the end, you'll have the tools to build a life that honors your unique identity and supports your well-being.

Rediscovering Personal Interests, Goals, and Values

Many people who struggle with codependency have spent so much time focused on others that they've lost touch with their own interests, values, and goals. Rediscovering these aspects of yourself is essential for building a fulfilling life, as it helps you understand what brings you joy, meaning, and purpose.

Recognizing the Impact of Codependency on Your Identity

When codependency takes hold, it often leads to a state of "identity fusion," where your sense of self becomes intertwined with others' needs and expectations. You may find that your thoughts, decisions, and actions are shaped by a desire to please, support, or maintain harmony rather than reflecting your true self. Recognizing this impact allows you to approach the process of reclaiming your identity with compassion and patience.

Exercise: Exploring Your Core Values and Interests

Reconnecting with your core values and interests is an essential first step in rediscovering your identity. This exercise will help you clarify what matters most to you and where your passions lie.

1. **Identify Your Core Values:** Take a few moments to reflect on the qualities or principles that matter most to you. Write down five to ten values that resonate with you deeply. Examples might include honesty, creativity, kindness, freedom, or personal growth.

2. **Reflect on Your Passions:** Think back to activities or topics that you've enjoyed in the past, even if they're things you haven't done recently. What brings you excitement, curiosity, or fulfillment? Write down any hobbies, interests, or pursuits that come to mind.

3. **Ask Yourself, "Why?":** For each value or interest, ask yourself why it's important to you. This will help deepen your

understanding and ensure that these choices come from your true self rather than external pressures or expectations.

4. **Identify Goals Aligned with Your Values:** Look at the values and interests you've identified and think about goals that reflect them. For example, if one of your values is personal growth, a goal might be to read a book on self-development each month. If creativity is a passion, you might set a goal to start a new artistic project.

This exercise helps you begin to reconnect with your unique values, passions, and goals, giving you a foundation for building a life that truly reflects who you are.

Crafting a Life Plan That Reflects Your True Self and Desires

Once you've identified your values, interests, and goals, the next step is to create a plan that aligns with your authentic self. A life plan is a roadmap that guides your choices, helping you make decisions that honor your true desires and priorities. This plan doesn't have to be rigid or detailed; instead, it's a flexible guide that evolves as you grow.

Steps to Crafting a Life Plan

1. **Define Your Vision:** Start by imagining the life you want to create. Visualize what a fulfilling, balanced life looks like for you. Consider the qualities, experiences, and relationships that would bring you the most joy and satisfaction. Write down your vision in a few sentences.

2. **Set Short- and Long-Term Goals:** Based on your vision, identify specific goals you'd like to achieve in the short term (within the next few months) and long-term (within the next few years). These goals should reflect your values and

desires, moving you closer to the life you envision.

3. **Break Goals into Actionable Steps:** For each goal, outline small, actionable steps that will help you make progress. For example, if a long-term goal is to start a new career, a short-term step might be researching educational programs or networking within your field of interest.

4. **Create a Timeline:** Establish a realistic timeline for each goal. Set motivating but flexible deadlines, allowing room for adjustment if needed.

5. **Identify Potential Challenges and Solutions:** Consider any obstacles that might arise as you work toward your goals, and brainstorm solutions or strategies to overcome them. This proactive approach helps you stay focused and resilient.

6. **Review and Adjust Regularly:** A life plan is not set in stone. Set aside time every few months to review your goals, track your progress, and make adjustments as needed. As you grow, your goals may shift, and that's okay.

Crafting a life plan helps you take ownership of your future and create a meaningful path that aligns with your authentic self. By setting intentional goals and taking actionable steps, you build a life that reflects your deepest values and aspirations.

Strengthening Self-Esteem and Autonomy

Reclaiming your identity and autonomy requires a foundation of self-esteem, as well as the confidence to make choices independently. Self-esteem is the belief in your own worth and abilities, while autonomy is the ability to act on your own values and preferences without undue influence from others. Together, they empower you to live authentically, trusting your own decisions and honoring your needs.

Building Self-Esteem

Strengthening self-esteem involves shifting your focus from external validation to internal validation, recognizing that your worth is inherent and does not depend on others' approval

.

Exercise: Self-Affirmation Practice

Self-affirmations are positive statements that reinforce your worth, resilience, and unique qualities. By practicing affirmations regularly, you can reprogram self-doubt and replace it with confidence and self-love.

1. **Identify Positive Qualities:** List five to ten qualities you admire about yourself. These might include traits like kindness, creativity, resilience, or compassion.
2. **Create Affirmations:** Turn each quality into an affirmation. For example, if one of your qualities is kindness, your affirmation might be, "I am kind and compassionate, and I bring warmth to those around me."
3. **Repeat Daily:** Spend a few minutes each morning or evening repeating these affirmations to yourself. Look in the mirror as you say them, and allow yourself to fully absorb the words.

Over time, affirmations help reinforce your self-worth, making it easier to act from a place of confidence rather than insecurity.

Cultivating Autonomy

Autonomy is the ability to make independent choices that reflect your values and priorities. For those with codependent tendencies, developing autonomy involves stepping away from people-pleasing behaviors and learning to trust your own judgment.

Exercise: Daily Autonomy Check-In

This exercise encourages you to practice autonomy by making small, independent choices throughout your day.

1. **Set a Daily Intention:** Each morning, set an intention to make at least one decision based on your own needs and desires. This could be as simple as choosing an activity that brings you joy or setting a boundary with someone.

2. **Pause Before Responding:** Whenever you're asked for help, a favor, or an invitation, pause and ask yourself, "Is this something I truly want to do?" Give yourself permission to say "no" if it doesn't align with your needs.

3. **Reflect at the End of the Day:** In the evening, take a few minutes to reflect on any decisions you made independently. Celebrate each choice, no matter how small, that honored your autonomy.

Practicing autonomy helps you build a stronger sense of self-trust, empowering you to make choices that support your well-being and authenticity.

Creating a Daily Routine to Support Identity and Autonomy

Integrating these practices into your daily routine helps reinforce your reclaimed identity and autonomy, allowing you to live authentically and confidently. Here are some ideas for creating a daily routine that supports your journey:

1. **Morning Intentions for Authentic Living**

Start your day with an intention that reflects your commitment to living authentically. This could be as simple as, "Today, I will honor my needs," or "I will make choices that reflect my values." Setting an intention grounds you in your identity, guiding your decisions and interactions throughout the day.

2. **Midday Check-In for Self-Awareness**

Take a brief pause during the day to check in with yourself. Notice how you're feeling, any challenges you've encountered, and whether your actions align with your values. Use this check-in to make adjustments as needed, ensuring that you stay connected to your true self.

3. **Evening Reflection on Autonomy and Growth**

At the end of the day, spend a few minutes reflecting on your progress. Consider any moments where you prioritized your needs, asserted your boundaries, or acted from a place of autonomy. Acknowledge these achievements and celebrate the ways you honored your identity and autonomy.

Embracing the Journey of Self-Discovery

Reclaiming your identity and autonomy is an ongoing journey of self-discovery. Each choice you make to prioritize your needs, act on your values, and pursue your goals strengthens your sense of self and empowers you to live authentically. This process isn't about perfection; it's about progress, allowing yourself to grow and evolve while staying true to who you are.

As you continue this journey, remember to approach yourself with compassion, patience, and curiosity. Rediscovering your identity and building autonomy may feel challenging at times, but each step forward brings you closer to a life that genuinely reflects your values, desires, and unique strengths.

Moving Forward

Reclaiming your identity and autonomy is a powerful act of self-liberation. By rediscovering your values, crafting a life plan, and strengthening your self-esteem, you're building a foundation for a life that honors your authentic self. This newfound independence will empower you to engage in relationships and experiences from a place of confidence and fulfillment.

In the next chapter, we'll explore how to identify healthy versus unhealthy relationship patterns, enabling you to create connections that support your growth and well-being. By building relationships that align with your values, you'll find even greater strength in your journey of self-discovery and emotional freedom.

PART IV

Chapter 11

Identifying Healthy vs. Unhealthy Relationships

AS YOU RECLAIM YOUR IDENTITY AND BUILD emotional independence, a key aspect of maintaining this progress lies in your relationships. Relationships are a fundamental part of life, offering companionship, support, and growth. However, not all relationships are created equal. Some relationships uplift and strengthen you, while others may hold you back, drain your energy, or even harm your well-being. Recognizing the difference between healthy and unhealthy relationship patterns is essential to creating connections that support your growth and healing.

In this chapter, we'll explore the characteristics of balanced, supportive relationships and discuss how to identify when a relationship is contributing to your personal growth versus when it's hindering it. By understanding these patterns, you'll be better equipped to make conscious choices about who you allow into your life and how you engage with them. Ultimately, cultivating healthy relationships can enhance your journey of self-discovery, emotional independence, and fulfillment.

Characteristics of Balanced, Supportive Relationships

Healthy relationships provide a foundation of mutual respect, trust, and support. In these relationships, both individuals feel valued, safe, and free to express themselves authentically. A balanced, supportive relationship is one in which both people contribute equally, respect each other's boundaries, and encourage each other's growth.

Key Characteristics of Healthy Relationships

1. **Mutual Respect:** Respect is the foundation of any healthy relationship. Both individuals value each other's thoughts, feelings, and boundaries. There's no need to "prove" worthiness or win approval, as each person feels respected for who they are.

2. **Open and Honest Communication:** Healthy relationships thrive on clear and open communication. Both people feel comfortable expressing their feelings, concerns, and needs without fear of judgment or backlash. Active listening and empathy are integral parts of communication, allowing each person to feel heard and understood.

3. **Support for Personal Growth:** In a supportive relationship, both people encourage each other's growth, dreams, and goals. They celebrate each other's successes and provide comfort during challenging times, recognizing that personal growth benefits both the individual and the relationship.

4. **Balanced Give-and-Take:** Healthy relationships involve an equitable exchange of support, care, and effort. Both individuals feel comfortable giving and receiving, and there is no sense of imbalance or obligation. Each person feels appreciated, not taken for granted.

5. **Trust and Dependability:** Trust is essential for a secure, lasting relationship. In a healthy relationship, both people trust each other's intentions and actions, knowing they can rely on one another. They follow through on promises, creating a sense of security and dependability.

6. **Healthy Boundaries:** Healthy relationships honor and respect boundaries. Each person understands that boundaries are necessary for maintaining individuality, self-respect, and emotional well-being. Boundaries are not seen as threats but as essential for personal freedom and respect.

7. **Emotional Safety and Vulnerability:** In a balanced relationship, both people feel safe to be vulnerable and express their emotions. There's a sense of emotional safety where each person can be authentic, share their fears and insecurities, and know they'll be met with compassion, not judgment.

8. **Conflict Resolution with Respect:** Disagreements are natural in any relationship, but in a healthy one, conflicts are handled respectfully. Both people approach conflicts with a desire to understand each other's perspective, work toward a solution, and avoid blame, criticism, or contempt.

These characteristics form the foundation of a healthy relationship, providing an environment where both people can flourish, individually and together. While no relationship is perfect, these qualities create a supportive dynamic that fosters mutual respect, emotional safety, and growth.

Recognizing When Relationships Serve Growth

Healthy relationships support and encourage your journey of self-discovery, emotional independence, and personal development.

They offer a positive space where you can explore your true self, pursue your goals, and become the best version of yourself. Here are some signs that a relationship is serving your growth:

1. You Feel Empowered to Be Yourself

In a growth-oriented relationship, you feel free to express your authentic self without fear of judgment. You don't feel pressured to change or conform to someone else's expectations. Instead, you're encouraged to embrace your uniqueness and pursue your passions.

2. Your Independence is Respected

A relationship that serves your growth respects your autonomy. You can maintain your interests, friendships, and personal goals without feeling guilty or pressured to prioritize the relationship above everything else. The relationship adds to your life without diminishing your individuality.

3. You're Challenged in a Positive Way

Growth-oriented relationships sometimes challenge you to step outside your comfort zone, try new things, or rethink limiting beliefs. This doesn't mean they pressure you to change; instead, they inspire you to expand your perspective and explore your potential.

4. You Feel Safe to Communicate Your Needs

In a supportive relationship, you can openly express your needs, desires, and boundaries without fear of conflict or rejection. Your partner or friend listens and respects what you share, fostering a sense of safety and trust.

5. There's Consistent Emotional Support

When relationships serve your growth, they provide consistent emotional support, especially during difficult times. You know you can rely on the other person for encouragement, empathy, and understanding, which helps you stay resilient and grounded.

Healthy relationships act as mirrors, reflecting back your strengths and supporting you in becoming the person you aspire to be. These relationships help you feel valued and fulfilled, enhancing your personal journey rather than detracting from it.

Recognizing When Relationships Hinder Growth

While some relationships support growth, others can hinder it, especially if they involve patterns of manipulation, dependency, or disrespect. Unhealthy relationships often drain your energy, erode your confidence, and make it difficult to prioritize your needs. Here are some signs that a relationship may be holding you back:

1. **You Feel Drained or Overwhelmed**

   Unhealthy relationships are often emotionally draining. You may feel exhausted, anxious, or overwhelmed after spending time with the other person, as though the relationship demands more energy than it gives.

2. **There's a Lack of Respect for Boundaries**

   In relationships that hinder growth, boundaries are frequently ignored or dismissed. You may feel guilty for setting boundaries, or the other person may react with anger or resistance, making it difficult to protect your well-being.

3. **You Feel Responsible for the Other Person's Emotions**

   Unhealthy relationships often involve emotional dependency, where one person feels responsible for managing the other's feelings or moods. You may find yourself "walking on eggshells" to avoid upsetting the other person, which can undermine your confidence and autonomy.

4. **There's a Power Imbalance**

   Relationships that hinder growth often involve a power imbalance, where one person holds control over decisions, resources, or emotional support. This imbalance can create a dynamic of dependency, making it difficult for you to assert your needs or pursue your own goals.

5. Communication is Often Negative or Defensive

Unhealthy relationships may involve frequent criticism, defensiveness, or contempt. You may feel judged or attacked for expressing your feelings, leading to resentment or self-doubt.

6. You Feel Isolated from Other Connections

In relationships that hinder growth, the other person may discourage you from maintaining outside relationships or pursuing individual interests. This isolation can lead to dependency, making it harder to leave or set boundaries in the relationship.

7. There's an Emphasis on Control Rather Than Support

In unhealthy relationships, one person may try to control the other's choices, behaviors, or appearance. Rather than supporting your growth and independence, the relationship may feel constricting, with an expectation to conform to the other person's needs or expectations.

If you recognize any of these signs, it may be worth re-evaluating the relationship to determine whether it's genuinely serving your well-being and personal growth. Recognizing unhealthy patterns empowers you to make informed choices about who you allow into your life and how you engage with them.

Moving from Unhealthy to Healthy Relationship Patterns

Shifting from unhealthy to healthy relationship patterns takes time and self-awareness. Here are some strategies to help you transition to more balanced, growth-oriented relationships:

1. **Establish Clear Boundaries**

Boundaries are essential for protecting your well-being and creating a balanced relationship. Communicate your boundaries openly, and be prepared to reinforce them consistently. Healthy relationships respect boundaries, while unhealthy relationships may resist or dismiss them.

2. **Prioritize Relationships That Uplift and Support You**

Surround yourself with people who encourage your growth, respect your individuality, and celebrate your successes. Seek out connections that bring you joy, positivity, and fulfillment, allowing you to thrive.

3. **Recognize and Break Free from Toxic Patterns**

Unhealthy relationship patterns can become ingrained over time. Recognize recurring patterns, such as people-pleasing or dependency, and take steps to break free from them. This might involve seeking support from a therapist, practicing assertive communication, or gradually detaching from relationships that hinder your growth.

4. **Focus on Self-Worth and Independence**

Healthy relationships start with a strong foundation of self-worth and independence. By cultivating a positive self-image and honoring your needs, you can engage in relationships from a place of confidence, reducing the likelihood of falling into unhealthy dynamics.

5. **Be Selective About Who You Allow into Your Life**

As you become more intentional about your relationships, it's important to be selective about who you allow into your inner circle. Choose people who align with your values, respect your boundaries, and contribute positively to your life.

Building healthy relationships is an ongoing process, but each step you take brings you closer to a life filled with connections that honor your identity, autonomy, and growth.

Reflecting on Your Relationships

Taking time to reflect on your relationships can help you clarify which connections support your growth and which may be holding you back.

Exercise: Relationship Reflection Journal

Use this exercise to assess the relationships in your life. It will help you identify those that enhance your well-being and those that may need re-evaluation.

1. **List Key Relationships:** Write down the names of people you interact with regularly, including family, friends, and romantic partners.

2. **Assess Each Relationship:** For each person, reflect on the following questions:

   • How do I feel after spending time with this person? Energized or drained?

   • Do I feel respected and supported in this relationship?

   • Does this person encourage my growth and individuality, or do they try to control or limit me?

   • Am I able to set boundaries in this relationship without fear of conflict?

3. **Identify Patterns:** Look for patterns across your relationships. Are there common traits among those who support your growth versus those who don't?

4. **Set Intentions:** Based on your reflections, set intentions for cultivating healthier dynamics in your relationships. This

might include setting new boundaries, prioritizing certain connections, or letting go of relationships that no longer serve you.

This reflection exercise allows you to gain clarity and make intentional choices about the relationships in your life, empowering you to foster connections that support your journey.

Moving Forward

Learning to recognize healthy versus unhealthy relationship patterns is a powerful step in building a life that reflects your true self. By surrounding yourself with people who support your growth, encourage your independence, and respect your boundaries, you create an environment where you can thrive, both individually and within your relationships.

In the next chapter, we'll explore communication and conflict resolution skills, equipping you with tools to navigate challenges and communicate effectively in all types of relationships. Each skill you develop brings you closer to a life filled with authentic, supportive connections that honor your worth and well-being.

Chapter 12

Communication & Conflict Resolution Skills

EFFECTIVE COMMUNICATION AND CONFLICT RESOLUTION SKILLS are essential components of healthy relationships. For those overcoming codependency, learning to communicate assertively and handle conflicts constructively can be transformative. Codependent patterns often include people-pleasing, passive communication, and avoidance of conflict. However, healthy relationships require open, honest communication and the ability to navigate disagreements respectfully.

In this chapter, we'll explore practical tips for assertive communication, strategies for navigating conflicts without falling into codependent habits, and exercises that encourage respectful disagreement and mutual understanding. By developing these skills, you can build stronger, more balanced relationships while maintaining your self-respect and boundaries.

Practical Tips for Assertive Communication

Assertive communication is a skill that allows you to express your thoughts, needs, and feelings openly and honestly while respecting others. It's a balanced approach that neither dominates nor minimizes your voice. For people recovering from codependency, assertive communication can feel challenging at first, but it's a skill that grows with practice.

What is Assertive Communication?

Assertive communication is a form of expression that values both your needs and the needs of others. It contrasts with passive communication, where you might suppress your thoughts or feelings to avoid conflict, and aggressive communication, where you may disregard others' needs to get your point across. Assertiveness strikes a balance, allowing you to stand up for yourself while remaining respectful.

Key characteristics of assertive communication include:

- **Directness:** Assertive communication involves stating your needs clearly and concisely, without ambiguity or "hinting."
- **Respect:** It respects both your needs and the other person's, aiming for a solution that works for everyone.
- **Confidence:** Assertive communicators speak with confidence, without apologizing for their feelings or downplaying their needs.

Techniques for Practicing Assertive Communication

Use "I" Statements: "I" statements allow you to express your feelings without sounding accusatory. For example, instead of saying, "You never listen to me," try, "I feel unheard when I don't get a chance to speak."

1. **Be Direct and Specific:** Instead of hinting at what you

want, be clear about your needs. For example, "I would appreciate it if we could split household chores equally" is more effective than saying, "It would be nice if you helped more around the house."

2. **Maintain Eye Contact and Open Body Language:** Nonverbal communication plays a significant role in assertiveness. Maintain gentle eye contact, keep your posture relaxed but confident, and avoid crossing your arms, which can appear defensive.

3. **Use a Calm, Steady Tone:** Keep your tone neutral and calm, even if you're discussing a difficult issue. Speaking with a steady tone helps convey confidence and self-assuredness.

4. **Acknowledge Others' Feelings:** Being assertive doesn't mean ignoring others' perspectives. For instance, you might say, "I understand that you're busy, but it's important to me that we spend some quality time together."

Practicing these techniques will make assertive communication feel more natural. They will empower you to express yourself openly while respecting your boundaries and the other person's needs.

Navigating Conflicts Without Falling into Codependent Habits

Conflict is a natural part of any relationship, but for those overcoming codependency, it can trigger people-pleasing behaviors or a fear of rejection. Navigating conflict constructively requires shifting from patterns of avoidance or self-sacrifice to approaches that prioritize open dialogue, respect, and mutual understanding.

Common Codependent Habits in Conflict

Understanding your default responses to conflict can help you break free from codependent patterns. Here are some everyday codependent habits and strategies for handling conflict more effectively:

- **People-Pleasing:** Codependent individuals often avoid conflict by giving in to others' demands or avoiding difficult topics, fearing rejection or disapproval.

- **Alternative Approach:** Instead of immediately agreeing to avoid conflict, take a pause and ask yourself, "What is my true opinion on this matter?" Give yourself permission to express it respectfully.

- **Passive Communication:** Many people with codependent tendencies adopt a passive approach in conflicts, suppressing their own needs to maintain harmony.

- **Alternative Approach:** Practice using assertive communication to express your needs. For example, if someone dismisses your perspective, respond with, "I understand your view, but my feelings on this matter are important as well."

- **Fear of Abandonment:** Some people may compromise their own needs during conflicts, fearing that standing up for themselves will lead to rejection.

- **Alternative Approach:** Remind yourself that healthy relationships can withstand disagreements. Conflicts do not define your worth, nor do they necessarily lead to abandonment.

By recognizing these codependent habits, you can approach conflict from a place of self-respect, aiming for a resolution that honors your needs as well as the relationship.

Steps for Navigating Conflict Constructively

1. **Pause Before Reacting:** When emotions run high, it's easy to respond impulsively. Take a few deep breaths before engaging in the conversation, allowing yourself a moment to gather your thoughts and approach the issue calmly.

2. **Express Your Perspective Clearly:** State your feelings and needs in a straightforward way. Use "I" statements to describe how you feel, and be specific about what you need or want.

3. **Listen Actively:** Give the other person a chance to share their perspective without interrupting. Show empathy by acknowledging their feelings, even if you disagree. For example, "I understand that you're frustrated, and I'd like to find a solution that works for both of us."

4. **Focus on the Issue, Not the Person:** Keep the focus on the issue at hand, avoiding personal attacks or generalizations. Instead of saying, "You always do this," focus on specific actions: "I felt hurt when my opinion was dismissed in the meeting."

5. **Look for Compromise and Collaboration:** Conflict resolution isn't about "winning" but finding a solution that respects both parties' needs. Be open to compromise and invite the other person to collaborate on a solution.

Approaching conflict with respect, openness, and a willingness to listen can lead to deeper understanding and stronger relationships. Remember that healthy conflict is a sign of a mature relationship, not a threat to it.

Exercises for Respectful Disagreement and Mutual Understanding

Respectful disagreement allows you to engage in constructive conversations, even when you have differing opinions. By practicing respectful disagreement, you develop the ability to maintain boundaries and mutual respect during challenging discussions, enhancing your communication skills and emotional resilience.

Exercise 1: Practice "Perspective-Taking" for Mutual Understanding

Perspective-taking involves putting yourself in the other person's shoes to understand their point of view better. This doesn't mean you have to agree with them, but it helps you approach the conversation with empathy.

1. **Reflect on Their Point of View:** Take a few moments to consider the other person's perspective. Ask yourself, "What might they be feeling or thinking right now?" or "What past experiences might be influencing their reaction?"

2. **Acknowledge Their Feelings:** In the conversation, acknowledge their feelings to show that you understand. For example, "I can see that this issue is important to you, and I appreciate you sharing your perspective with me."

3. **Share Your Own Perspective:** After acknowledging their viewpoint, share your perspective calmly and clearly, using "I" statements. For example, "I understand where you're coming from, and I'd like to share how I see it."

Perspective-taking promotes empathy, making it easier to navigate disagreements with respect and mutual understanding.

Exercise 2: The "Agree to Disagree" Technique

The "Agree to Disagree" technique is helpful when you realize that reaching a full agreement may not be possible. This approach allows both parties to respect each other's perspectives while accepting their differences.

1. **Acknowledge the Difference:** Clearly state that you recognize there are differences in your viewpoints. For example, "I see that we have different perspectives on this issue."

2. **Validate Each Other's Perspective:** Even if you don't agree, validate the other person's right to hold their opinion. Say something like, "I respect that you have your own view, and I appreciate you sharing it with me."

3. **Set Boundaries for Resolution:** If the issue cannot be fully resolved, agree to set it aside and move forward. For example, "Let's agree to disagree on this point and focus on finding a solution we're both comfortable with."

4. **Move Forward Respectfully:** Once you've agreed to disagree, shift the focus to maintaining respect and harmony in the relationship. Remind yourself that not all issues need to be resolved in the same way and that differing opinions don't define the entire relationship.

The "Agree to Disagree" technique allows you to navigate challenging discussions without the pressure of "winning," fostering a culture of respect and acceptance within your relationships.

Moving Forward with Communication and Conflict Resolution Skills

Developing communication and conflict resolution skills is a gradual process, but each step forward strengthens your ability to engage in relationships from a place of confidence and self-respect. By learning to communicate assertively, handle conflicts constructively, and engage in respectful disagreement, you create a foundation for healthy, balanced relationships that enhance your personal growth.

Remember that communication is a skill that improves with practice. Every conversation offers an opportunity to apply what you've learned, and over time, these skills will become second nature. Trust in your ability to navigate challenges gracefully, knowing that every step you take brings you closer to a life filled with fulfilling, supportive relationships.

In the next chapter, we'll explore trust-building and secure attachments, helping you create connections that provide a sense of safety, intimacy, and mutual respect. By fostering secure attachments, you can build relationships that enrich your life and reflect the progress you've made on your journey.

Chapter 13

Building Trust & Secure Attachments

DEVELOPING TRUST AND SECURE ATTACHMENTS is a vital step in creating healthy, fulfilling relationships. Secure attachment allows you to feel safe, supported, and valued in your connections with others while also empowering you to maintain your independence and self-worth. For those who have experienced codependency, building trust and creating secure attachments can feel challenging, especially if past relationships involved betrayal, manipulation, or emotional neglect. However, it's entirely possible to cultivate a secure attachment style as an adult, fostering connections that bring joy, security, and mutual respect.

In this chapter, we'll explore practical steps to develop a secure attachment style, address trust issues, and open up to intimacy in safe, healthy ways. By embracing these practices, you can create relationships that honor your well-being and allow you to experience deeper, more meaningful connections.

Understanding Secure Attachment in Adult Relationships

Attachment styles are patterns of relating to others that develop in early childhood, typically based on experiences with caregivers. While early attachment experiences shape how we relate to others, attachment styles are not fixed—they can evolve and change over time, especially with conscious effort and practice.

Characteristics of a Secure Attachment Style

A secure attachment style is characterized by feelings of safety, trust, and confidence in relationships. People with secure attachments are comfortable with intimacy and independence, and they engage in relationships from a place of self-worth and mutual respect. Here are some key traits of secure attachment:

1. Emotional Stability: Securely attached individuals can manage their emotions effectively. They feel comfortable expressing their needs and are open to hearing others' needs without feeling threatened.

2. Trust and Dependability: People with secure attachment styles trust their partners and friends and are comfortable depending on them. They trust that others will be there in times of need, and they themselves are reliable and supportive.

3. Comfort with Intimacy: Securely attached individuals feel safe with closeness and vulnerability. They can open up about their emotions, share their inner thoughts, and seek comfort from others when needed.

4. Healthy Boundaries: Secure attachment involves a balance between closeness and independence. Securely attached people can set and respect boundaries, maintaining their sense of self without losing connection with others.

5. Effective Conflict Resolution: When disagreements arise, securely attached people approach conflicts with empathy and respect. They're willing to listen, compromise, and work toward solutions without escalating the conflict.

These characteristics create a foundation of trust, mutual support, and respect in relationships, allowing both people to grow together while maintaining their individuality.

Steps to Develop a Secure Attachment Style in Adult Relationships

Here are steps for practicing specific behaviors and mindsets that will help promote emotional safety, trust, and resilience. These steps will help you develop a secure attachment style in your relationships:

1. Develop Self-Awareness and Emotional Regulation

Secure attachment begins with self-awareness and emotional regulation. Learning to recognize your emotions, manage them effectively, and respond thoughtfully in relationships creates a stable foundation for connection.

How to Practice Emotional Regulation:

- Pause Before Reacting: When emotions run high, take a few moments to breathe and calm yourself before responding. This helps prevent impulsive reactions and allows you to communicate more effectively.

- Identify Triggers: Notice situations that trigger intense emotions, such as fear of rejection or jealousy. Reflect on these triggers and explore whether they're rooted in past experiences.

- Practice Self-Soothing Techniques: Self-soothing methods, like deep breathing, visualization, or mindfulness, can help you regulate your emotions, allowing you to engage in relationships with a clear and balanced mind.

By managing your emotions, you reduce the risk of falling into reactive or anxious patterns, building a stronger foundation for secure attachments.

2. Communicate Needs Openly and Directly

Clear, direct communication is a cornerstone of secure attachment. Expressing your needs and feelings openly helps prevent misunderstandings, promotes mutual understanding, and fosters trust.

How to Practice Open Communication:

- **Use "I" Statements:** Communicate your feelings and needs using "I" statements, such as, "I feel [emotion] when [situation]." This approach prevents blaming and focuses on your experience.

- **Be Specific and Clear:** Instead of hinting or expecting others to read your mind, express your needs directly. For example, "I'd appreciate it if we could spend some quality time together this weekend."

- **Listen Actively:** Give your partner or friend the opportunity to share their feelings as well. Listening actively, without interrupting or judging, shows respect and fosters mutual understanding.

By communicating openly, you create an environment where both you and the other person feel comfortable sharing, leading to deeper connection and trust.

3. Practice Vulnerability Gradually

Opening up emotionally and allowing yourself to be vulnerable can feel challenging, especially if past experiences have led to betrayal or rejection. Practicing vulnerability gradually in a safe and trusting environment can help you build emotional intimacy without feeling overwhelmed.

How to Practice Gradual Vulnerability:

- **Start Small:** Begin by sharing something minor or lighthearted, such as a favorite memory or a personal goal. Notice how the other person responds and whether they show understanding.

- **Share Emotions Honestly:** As you feel more comfortable, gradually share deeper emotions or personal experiences. For instance, express how a particular event made you feel, or talk about a recent challenge you faced.

- **Acknowledge Your Feelings:** If you feel nervous about being vulnerable, it's okay to express this. Saying something like, "It feels a bit hard for me to share this, but I want to be open with you" can foster a sense of honesty and trust.

Building trust and intimacy takes time, and practicing vulnerability in small steps allows you to become more comfortable opening up in a safe and empowering way.

Healing Trust Issues and Opening Up to Intimacy

Trust is a critical component of secure attachments, but for those who have experienced betrayal, abuse, or emotional neglect, developing trust can feel daunting. Healing trust issues and opening up to intimacy involve both self-reflection and intentional action, creating space for safety, mutual respect, and emotional connection.

Understanding the Root of Trust Issues

Trust issues often stem from past experiences of betrayal, inconsistency, or neglect. These experiences can create a sense of hypervigilance, where you're constantly on the lookout for signs of potential harm or abandonment. Recognizing the origins of your trust issues helps you approach them with compassion, understanding that they're a natural response to previous pain.

Steps to Heal Trust Issues

1. **Acknowledge Past Experiences:** Reflect on experiences that led to your trust issues, such as broken promises, betrayals, or emotional neglect. Acknowledging these experiences helps you understand that your trust issues are a response to past pain, not a personal flaw.

2. **Challenge Fear-Based Beliefs:** Trust issues often create beliefs like "People always leave" or "I can't trust anyone." Challenge these beliefs by examining evidence in your current life. For example, notice friends or family members who have shown consistent support and dependability.

3. **Take Small Steps Toward Trust:** Start by placing trust in small ways. For example, rely on someone for a minor favor or share a small vulnerability. Gradually expand your trust as the person proves reliable, reinforcing your sense of safety.

4. **Set Boundaries to Protect Yourself:** Establishing boundaries helps you create a safe space to build trust. Boundaries provide protection, allowing you to engage in relationships without fear of being overwhelmed or overexposed.

Healing trust issues takes time and patience. Each step forward, no matter how small, helps rebuild your ability to trust, fostering a sense of security in your relationships.

Opening Up to Healthy Intimacy

Emotional intimacy is the ability to connect deeply with others, sharing your thoughts, feelings, and experiences in a supportive and understanding environment. For those with a history of codependency or trust issues, building intimacy may require overcoming fears of vulnerability and rejection.

Practicing Healthy Intimacy

1. **Set Intentions for Genuine Connection:** Approach relationships with the intention of forming authentic connections rather than seeking approval or validation. Focus on genuinely getting to know the other person and allowing them to know the real you.

2. **Balance Giving and Receiving:** Intimacy is a reciprocal process that involves both giving and receiving. Practice sharing your own thoughts and feelings while also showing curiosity and empathy toward the other person.

3. **Create Safe Spaces for Emotional Expression:** Foster an environment where both you and the other person feel comfortable expressing emotions without fear of judgment. Encourage open communication, where each person can share without feeling pressured or criticized.

4. **Respect Boundaries:** Intimacy flourishes when both individuals feel respected and secure. Honor each other's boundaries and avoid pushing for a deeper connection than feels comfortable.

Opening up to intimacy is a gradual process, allowing you to build deeper connections without sacrificing your emotional independence. Each experience of genuine connection reinforces your ability to form healthy, meaningful relationships.

Exercises for Building Trust and Secure Attachments

The following exercises are designed to help you build trust, foster secure attachments, and deepen your sense of connection in relationships. By practicing these exercises regularly, you can develop a stronger foundation for healthy, balanced relationships.

Exercise 1: The Trust-Building Journal

A trust-building journal is a simple way to document positive experiences in relationships, reinforcing evidence of trustworthiness and dependability.

1. **Document Positive Interactions:** Each day, write down moments in which someone showed trustworthiness, dependability, or support. For example, if a friend kept a promise or a partner listened attentively, note it in your journal.

2. **Reflect on the Experience:** Take a moment to reflect on how the positive interaction made you feel. Did you feel respected, valued, or supported?

3. **Acknowledge Patterns of Trust:** Over time, review your journal entries to recognize patterns of trust in your relationships. These reflections can help counterbalance past negative experiences and reinforce trust.

This exercise helps shift your focus toward positive aspects of relationships, creating a foundation for trust and secure attachment.

Exercise 2: Practicing Gratitude and Appreciation in Relationships

Expressing gratitude and appreciation strengthens bonds, promotes a positive atmosphere, and fosters secure attachment.

1. **Identify Something You Appreciate:** Reflect on one thing you genuinely appreciate about someone in your life. This could be their kindness, sense of humor, or dependability.

2. **Express Appreciation Directly:** Share your appreciation

with the person, either verbally or in a note. Be specific about what you value and how it impacts you. For example, "I really appreciate how you always listen to me; it makes me feel supported."

3. **Notice Their Reaction:** Observe how the person responds to your appreciation. Often, expressing gratitude creates a positive feedback loop, where both people feel valued and secure.

Practicing gratitude deepens emotional bonds, promoting a sense of safety, trust, and appreciation in your relationships.

Moving Forward with Trust and Secure Attachments

Building trust and secure attachments is a journey of self-awareness, patience, and resilience. Each step forward allows you to experience deeper, more meaningful connections, free from the patterns of dependency or fear that may have held you back in the past. By focusing on emotional regulation, open communication, and healthy intimacy, you create relationships that provide both support and independence, fostering a foundation of mutual respect and fulfillment.

Remember, building secure attachments is a gradual process. Be patient with yourself and celebrate each step toward greater trust and connection. As you develop these skills, relationships will become a source of strength, joy, and stability, enriching your journey of self-discovery and emotional independence.

In the next chapter, we'll explore coping strategies for long-term healing, equipping you with tools to handle setbacks and continue nurturing your growth. Each chapter builds on the foundation of self-worth, trust, and resilience, empowering you to create a life that reflects your authentic self and values.

PART V

Chapter 14

Coping Strategies For Long-Term Healing

As you continue on the journey to overcome codependency and build healthier relationships, it's essential to have strategies in place for maintaining your progress and handling setbacks. Healing is not always a linear process; it's natural to encounter moments of difficulty, self-doubt, or even relapse into old patterns. However, with effective coping strategies, you can navigate these challenges with resilience, self-compassion, and confidence.

In this chapter, we'll explore tools for managing setbacks and difficult emotions, methods to prevent relapse into codependent behaviors, and the importance of developing a support network and maintaining positive influences. These strategies are designed to help you stay on course, deepen your growth, and create a sustainable path toward long-term healing and self-discovery.

Tools for Handling Setbacks and Difficult Emotions

Healing from codependency involves confronting emotions that may have been buried or minimized in the past, including fear, sadness, guilt, or shame. While it's natural to feel overwhelmed by these emotions at times, learning to handle them constructively is key to maintaining progress.

Accepting and Normalizing Setbacks

Setbacks are a normal part of growth. They don't signify failure or a return to square one; instead, they are opportunities to practice the skills you've learned and reinforce your progress. A setback might look like slipping back into people-pleasing tendencies, struggling with self-doubt, or experiencing anxiety in relationships. These moments are a chance to revisit your tools, exercise self-compassion, and recommit to your journey.

How to Normalize Setbacks:

- **Acknowledge the Setback:** Recognize that setbacks are part of the healing process and do not define your progress. Remind yourself that healing isn't linear, and setbacks are a chance to strengthen your skills.
- **Practice Self-Compassion:** Treat yourself with kindness and patience during setbacks. Instead of criticizing yourself, remind yourself that setbacks are a natural part of learning and growth.
- **Reflect on the Lesson:** Each setback can teach you something valuable. Reflect on what may have triggered the setback and consider how you can approach similar situations differently in the future.

Techniques for Managing Difficult Emotions

Emotions like fear, sadness, or guilt can arise unexpectedly, especially during challenging situations or moments of vulnerability. Here are some practical techniques for managing these emotions effectively:

1. **Mindful Observation:** Mindfulness helps you observe your emotions without judgment. When you feel a difficult emotion, pause and acknowledge it. Notice how it feels in your body and mind without trying to suppress or escape it. For example, if you feel anxious, say to yourself, "I'm feeling anxious right now," and take a few deep breaths.

2. **Emotional Labeling:** Putting a name to your emotions can help you process them more effectively. Simply identifying the emotion, such as "I'm feeling overwhelmed," can make it feel less overpowering. This practice creates space between you and the emotion, allowing you to respond rather than react.

3. **Practice Grounding Techniques:** Grounding exercises help bring you back to the present moment, reducing the intensity of overwhelming emotions. Try the 5-4-3-2-1 technique, where you identify five things you can see, four things you can touch, three things you can hear, two things you can smell, and one thing you can taste.

4. **Reframe Self-Talk:** When difficult emotions arise, it's easy to fall into negative self-talk. Challenge this by replacing critical thoughts with compassionate statements. Instead of thinking, "I'm failing," remind yourself, "This is a challenging moment, but I am learning and growing."

5. **Seek Support:** Don't hesitate to reach out to a trusted friend, family member, or therapist when you're struggling with difficult emotions. Sharing your feelings with someone who understands can provide relief and perspective.

These techniques empower you to manage emotions constructively, helping you maintain stability and confidence even during challenging times.

Methods to Prevent Relapse into Codependent Patterns

One of the most common challenges in long-term healing from codependency is the risk of falling back into old patterns. People-pleasing, dependency, and neglecting one's own needs can resurface, especially during stressful situations or in relationships with individuals who expect you to prioritize their needs. Being proactive and mindful can prevent these patterns from reasserting themselves.

Common Triggers for Codependent Behaviors

Identifying potential triggers for codependent patterns can help you take preventive action. Common triggers include:

- **Stressful Situations:** Stress often brings out old coping mechanisms, such as people-pleasing or avoiding conflict, as a way to maintain peace or gain reassurance.
- **Insecure Relationships:** Unhealthy or inconsistent relationships may trigger codependent behaviors as you attempt to "fix" the relationship or seek approval.
- **High-Stakes Situations:** When you fear rejection or disapproval, you may feel tempted to revert to codependent habits, like prioritizing others' needs over your own.

Recognizing these triggers allows you to prepare and respond more thoughtfully, reducing the likelihood of relapse.

Strategies to Prevent Codependent Relapse

Set and Reinforce Boundaries: Boundaries are essential for maintaining your sense of self and autonomy. Practice setting clear boundaries with others, and remind yourself that your needs and well-being are essential. If someone crosses a boundary, calmly reinforce it, even if it feels uncomfortable.

1. **Regularly Check in with Your Needs:** Take time each day to check in with yourself. Ask yourself, "What do I need right now?" and honor that need, whether it's rest, connection, or alone time. Prioritizing your needs consistently reduces the likelihood of self-neglect.

2. **Practice Self-Validation:** Codependent patterns often stem from a desire for external validation. Practice self-validation by acknowledging your own efforts, achievements, and feelings without needing others' approval. For example, after a challenging day, tell yourself, "I'm proud of myself for handling that situation with integrity."

3. **Challenge People-Pleasing Thoughts:** When you feel the urge to please others at your own expense, pause and ask yourself if this action aligns with your values and well-being. Remember that saying "no" or setting limits is a sign of self-respect, not selfishness.

4. **Reflect on Your Progress Regularly:** Take time each week or month to reflect on your progress and acknowledge any steps you've taken toward healthier relationships and self-care. This practice helps reinforce your commitment to long-term healing and reduces the appeal of old patterns.

By staying mindful and proactive, you can prevent relapse into codependent behaviors, ensuring that your relationships and choices align with your true self.

Developing a Support Network and Maintaining Positive Influences

Having a support network is crucial for long-term healing, as it provides encouragement, understanding, and accountability. A support network doesn't need to be large; even a few positive, reliable people in your life can make a significant difference. Surrounding yourself with positive influences helps reinforce your progress, offering you a safe space to express yourself and receive guidance.

Types of Support in a Healing Journey

1. **Emotional Support:** Emotional supporters are people who listen without judgment, offer empathy, and provide comfort during difficult times. They might be friends, family members, or a therapist who can hold space for your emotions.

2. **Accountability Support:** Accountability partners help you stay committed to your goals. This could be someone who checks in on your progress, reminds you of your boundaries, or encourages you to prioritize self-care.

3. **Guidance and Mentorship:** Mentors or role models provide valuable insight and advice. They may have experience overcoming similar challenges and can offer perspective, encouragement, and practical tools.

4. **Community Support:** Support groups, online communities, or therapy groups provide a sense of belonging and shared experience. In these spaces, you can connect with others who understand your journey and can offer mutual support.

Creating a well-rounded support network allows you to access different types of help when you need it, making it easier to navigate challenges and stay on course.

Steps to Build and Strengthen Your Support Network

1. **Identify Trusted Individuals:** Think about people in your

life who have demonstrated reliability, empathy, and respect for your boundaries. These are individuals who genuinely want to see you thrive and are willing to support your journey.

2. **Set Expectations:** Communicate openly with your support network about your needs. Let them know what kind of support you're looking for, whether it's emotional support, accountability, or guidance. Clear expectations create a stronger foundation for mutual understanding.

3. **Seek Out New Connections:** If you're looking to expand your support network, consider joining groups, workshops, or communities that align with your values and goals. This could include support groups for codependency, self-help workshops, or online forums for personal growth.

4. **Be Open to Giving and Receiving Support:** Healthy support networks are built on reciprocity. Be willing to offer support when possible and allow yourself to receive help without guilt. Remember that both giving and receiving support strengthen connections and contribute to a positive dynamic.

5. **Regularly Connect with Supportive People:** Make it a priority to connect with your support network regularly. This could be through weekly check-ins, phone calls, or occasional get-togethers. Consistent connection helps reinforce your growth and provides ongoing encouragement.

Building and nurturing a solid support network is an investment in your long-term healing, giving you access to guidance, encouragement, and positive influences that enhance your journey.

Maintaining Positive Influences in Your Life

In addition to developing a support network, maintaining positive influences is crucial for long-term growth. Positive influences are people, activities, and environments that inspire and uplift you, contributing to your sense of well-being and fulfillment.

Identifying Positive Influences

Consider the people and activities in your life that have a positive impact on you. Positive influences might include:

- **Friends Who Inspire Growth:** People who encourage your goals, respect your boundaries, and bring joy to your life.
- **Activities That Bring Fulfillment:** Hobbies or interests that align with your values, allowing you to express your creativity, curiosity, or passion.
- **Environments That Foster Peace:** Spaces that make you feel comfortable, safe, and relaxed, whether it's a cozy corner of your home, a favorite park, or a peaceful coffee shop.

Reflecting on these influences helps you identify areas of your life that support your well-being, giving you direction on how to prioritize them.

Strategies for Maintaining Positive Influences

1. **Prioritize Quality Time:** Make time for the people and activities that positively impact your life. Prioritizing quality time with supportive friends, engaging in fulfilling hobbies, or visiting environments that bring you peace reinforces your commitment to self-care.

2. **Limit Exposure to Negative Influences:** Be mindful of people or situations that drain your energy, diminish your

confidence, or trigger codependent behaviors. Limit your exposure to these influences and set boundaries to protect your well-being.

3. **Incorporate Positive Habits into Your Routine:** Identify small habits that bring positivity into your daily life. This might include morning meditation, journaling, or a daily walk in nature. Incorporating these habits into your routine can provide a consistent source of support and encouragement.

4. **Seek Out Opportunities for Growth:** Surround yourself with experiences that foster personal growth. This could involve taking a class, joining a community, or exploring a new hobby. Embracing growth-oriented activities helps you stay motivated and inspired.

By maintaining positive influences, you create a life reflecting your values, priorities, and self-worth. These influences reinforce your growth, making it easier to stay committed to long-term healing.

Moving Forward with Long-Term Healing

Long-term healing from codependency requires resilience, self-awareness, and a commitment to self-care. By equipping yourself with coping strategies for handling setbacks, preventing relapse, and building a strong support network, you empower yourself to navigate challenges with confidence and grace.

Remember that healing is an ongoing process, one that involves patience and compassion. Each step forward, each moment of self-awareness, and each connection with a supportive influence contribute to a stronger foundation of self-worth, resilience, and emotional freedom.

In the final chapter, we'll discuss how to create a life of emotional freedom, balancing self-care, growth, and fulfillment. Together, these final steps will guide you toward a life of independence, self-empowerment, and genuine happiness.

Chapter 15

Creating a Life of Emotional Freedom

CONGRATULATIONS ON REACHING THIS POINT IN YOUR JOURNEY! By exploring codependency, cultivating self-awareness, setting boundaries, and fostering healthy relationships, you've laid a strong foundation for lasting change. The final step in your recovery journey is learning to create a life of emotional freedom—a life in which you're guided by your values, empowered by your inner strength, and free from the need for external validation.

Emotional freedom is about more than just breaking away from codependent patterns; it's about building a life that reflects who you truly are. In this chapter, we'll define what success in recovery and emotional freedom look like, discuss strategies for living a balanced life centered on self-care, and share inspiring examples of individuals who have successfully overcome codependency.

Defining Success in Recovery: What Emotional Freedom Looks Like

Success in recovery looks different for everyone, as each person's journey and goals are unique. However, emotional freedom often includes several common elements that reflect self-assurance, independence, and a commitment to personal growth.

Key Characteristics of Emotional Freedom

1. **Self-Trust and Inner Confidence:** Emotional freedom means trusting yourself to make decisions that align with your values, needs, and boundaries. You no longer rely on others to validate your worth or approve of your choices, as you trust your own judgment.

2. **Balanced Relationships:** In a life of emotional freedom, relationships are balanced, supportive, and respectful. You engage with others from a place of mutual respect and feel free to express yourself without fear of rejection or abandonment.

3. **Emotional Resilience:** Emotional freedom includes the ability to manage difficult emotions, navigate setbacks, and bounce back from challenges. You can face difficult feelings without being overwhelmed, knowing that you have the tools to take care of yourself.

4. **Commitment to Self-Care:** Self-care is a priority in a life of emotional freedom. You actively make time for activities that nourish your mind, body, and soul, understanding that self-care is not selfish but essential.

5. **Authenticity and Self-Expression:** Emotional freedom involves embracing your authentic self, including your quirks, dreams, and individuality. You no longer feel the need to hide or conform to others' expectations, as you're comfortable being true to yourself.

6. **Purpose and Fulfillment:** Emotional freedom often comes with a sense of purpose and fulfillment. You find

meaning in your pursuits, whether through relationships, work, hobbies, or personal growth, and you're driven by your own goals rather than others' expectations.

These characteristics reflect a life in which you feel empowered, content, and secure in your sense of self. Emotional freedom isn't about never experiencing challenges or negative emotions; it's about developing the strength and resilience to navigate life on your terms.

Tips for Living a Balanced Life with Self-Care at the Forefront

Living a balanced life with self-care at the core is essential to sustaining emotional freedom. This approach allows you to nurture your well-being while enjoying fulfilling relationships, meaningful activities, and personal growth.

Prioritizing Self-Care: Mind, Body, and Spirit

1. **Physical Self-Care:** Taking care of your body is vital to emotional freedom, as physical health impacts mental and emotional well-being. Make time for regular exercise, sufficient sleep, and nutritious meals. Engage in activities that bring you joy, such as dancing, hiking, or practicing yoga. Physical self-care helps you feel energized, focused, and resilient.

2. **Emotional Self-Care:** Emotional self-care involves acknowledging, processing, and managing your feelings. Practice mindfulness, journaling, or talking with a trusted friend or therapist to navigate your emotions constructively. Give yourself permission to experience your feelings fully, without judgment, and prioritize activities that bring you joy, peace, or relaxation.

3. **Mental Self-Care:** Mental self-care helps you stay grounded, clear-minded, and focused on your goals. Engage in activities that stimulate your mind, such as reading, solving puzzles, or learning a new skill. Mental self-care also includes setting healthy boundaries around information intake—limit exposure to negative news, social media, or anything that causes unnecessary stress.

4. **Spiritual Self-Care:** Spiritual self-care means connecting with your inner values, beliefs, or a sense of purpose. This could involve meditation, prayer, spending time in nature, or engaging in creative practices. Nurturing your spirit enhances your sense of fulfillment, grounding you in values that reflect your authentic self.

Tips for Maintaining Balance in Everyday Life

1. **Set Realistic Goals and Expectations:** Set goals that reflect your current needs, energy levels, and priorities. Avoid putting too much pressure on yourself, and remember that progress doesn't require perfection. Celebrate each step forward, no matter how small, and adjust your goals as needed to stay aligned with your well-being.

2. **Practice Saying "No":** Saying "no" is essential for protecting your energy and boundaries. When you're asked to take on additional responsibilities, consider whether it aligns with your values and priorities. Saying "no" to others often means saying "yes" to yourself, allowing you to focus on what truly matters.

3. **Embrace Flexibility and Adaptability:** Life is dynamic, and sometimes, plans or routines need to shift. Embrace

flexibility as part of a balanced life, allowing yourself to adapt to changing circumstances without guilt. If something doesn't go as planned, remind yourself that you can adjust, recalibrate, and continue moving forward.

4. **Schedule Regular "Me" Time:** Carve out regular time for yourself each week. Whether it's a solo walk, a creative activity, or quiet reflection, "me" time allows you to recharge, reflect, and reconnect with your inner self.

5. **Check In with Yourself Regularly:** Take a few minutes each day to check in with yourself. Ask questions like, "How am I feeling?" and "What do I need right now?" Self-check-ins help you stay attuned to your needs and reinforce your commitment to self-care.

6. **Nurture Positive Relationships:** Surround yourself with people who uplift and inspire you. Cultivate relationships that respect your boundaries, honor your growth, and provide mutual support. Positive connections are a source of joy, encouragement, and balance, enriching your journey of emotional freedom.

Maintaining a balanced life with self-care at the forefront empowers you to live authentically and fully, prioritizing well-being and fulfillment without compromising your independence.

Inspiring Examples of Individuals Who Have Overcome Codependency

To illustrate what emotional freedom can look like, here are examples of individuals who have transformed their lives by overcoming codependency. These stories show that, while the journey may be challenging, the rewards are profound and deeply fulfilling.

Example 1: Sarah's Journey to Authenticity

Sarah was a dedicated caregiver and people-pleaser, always prioritizing others' needs and neglecting her own. She struggled with setting boundaries and felt that her worth was tied to how much she could give. After realizing how exhausted and unfulfilled she felt, Sarah began her journey to overcome codependency.

Through therapy and self-reflection, Sarah learned to identify her values, set boundaries, and communicate her needs assertively. She made time to rediscover her long-neglected hobbies, set career goals, and nurtured relationships that respected her boundaries. Today, Sarah feels confident, empowered, and free to be herself. Her relationships are balanced, and she finds joy in expressing her true self, knowing that she no longer needs to please everyone to feel valuable.

Example 2: Jason's Path to Self-Worth and Independence

Jason was raised in a family that depended on him for emotional support, and he carried this sense of responsibility into adulthood. In his professional life, he often took on others' tasks as his own and found it difficult to detach emotionally. Jason's turning point came when he realized that he was suffering from burnout, having neglected his own needs and sacrificed his well-being for others in his work life.

Jason began working with a support group and practiced self-soothing techniques, boundary-setting, and self-validation. He learned to prioritize his needs and let go of the guilt he felt for not "fixing" others' problems. Today, Jason feels a deep sense of self-worth and independence. He maintains supportive relationships, respects his boundaries, and experiences emotional freedom, knowing that he is worthy and whole on his own.

Example 3: Cara's Transformation from Dependency to Empowerment

Cara had always relied on her romantic relationships for validation, feeling lost without a partner. She feared being alone and struggled with self-doubt. Cara's breakthrough came when, after a particularly painful breakup, she began the work to recognize her pattern of dependency and started on the steps toward healing.

Cara focused on building a strong sense of self through self-compassion, hobbies, and friendships. She took time to reconnect with her values and passions, discovering her love for painting and yoga. With time, Cara found fulfillment within herself and no longer needed a relationship to feel complete. She now enters relationships from a place of wholeness, enjoying companionship without sacrificing her independence.

These stories show that emotional freedom is achievable, even for those who have struggled with codependency for many years. By embracing self-care, setting boundaries, and cultivating self-worth, each of these individuals created a life that reflects their true selves, free from the constraints of dependency.

Embracing Emotional Freedom as a Lifelong Journey

Creating a life of emotional freedom is an ongoing journey that involves growth, resilience, and self-compassion. While challenges may still arise, each step you've taken to overcome codependency strengthens your ability to handle them confidently. Here are some guiding principles to carry with you as you continue this journey:

1. **Stay Connected to Your Values:** Let your values serve as your compass. When making decisions, ask yourself if they align with what matters most to you. Living in alignment with your values helps you stay true to yourself and fosters

fulfillment.

2. **Keep Learning and Growing:** Personal growth is a life-long process. Embrace learning as part of your journey, whether through new experiences, relationships, or skills. Growth keeps you engaged with life and enriches your sense of purpose.

3. **Celebrate Progress, Not Perfection:** Remember that healing is not about being perfect; it's about progress. Celebrate each step forward, each boundary set, and each moment of self-care. Recognize that growth involves both successes and setbacks, and both are valuable.

4. **Practice Gratitude:** Gratitude helps you focus on the positive aspects of your journey, reinforcing your sense of fulfillment. Take time each day to acknowledge something you're grateful for, whether it's a supportive relationship, a personal achievement, or a moment of peace.

5. **Trust Yourself and Your Path:** Trust in your resilience, intuition, and ability to navigate life's ups and downs. Trust that you're equipped to handle whatever comes your way and that you have the strength to create a life that reflects your true self.

As you embrace emotional freedom, you'll find that life becomes richer, more meaningful, and deeply fulfilling. By prioritizing self-care, maintaining positive relationships, and living authentically, you've set the stage for a life of joy, purpose, and lasting inner peace.

As you reach the end of this book, take a moment to reflect on the journey you've undertaken. You've shown incredible courage and resilience, moving through self-discovery, healing, and growth with commitment and heart. The tools you now possess—self-awareness, emotional independence, and the ability to set boundaries—will continue to support you as you create a life that honors your true self. Remember, healing is a journey, not a destination, and each day offers a new opportunity to embrace your worth, pursue your passions, and nurture relationships that uplift you. Trust in the strength and wisdom you've cultivated, and know that you have the power to shape a future that brings you joy, fulfillment, and peace. Thank you for embarking on this journey, and may it bring you the freedom, happiness, and empowerment you deserve.

What's Next?

Use the **Companion Workbook** for Further Insight: If you haven't already, explore **Breaking Free of Codependency: A Holistic Guide to Healing, Emotional Resilience, and Self-Empowerment Companion Workbook** for deeper practices into the knowledge you've learned here.

Please consider leaving a review for this book, both to help us reach more readers as well as consider your valuable feedback. Thank you!

FURTHER READING

MANY OF THE CONCEPTS IN THIS BOOK are inspired by the foundational work of experts in psychology, trauma, attachment theory, and personal growth. Books like Codependent No More by Melody Beattie and Facing Codependence by Pia Mellody laid the groundwork for understanding codependency and its impact on relationships. Likewise, The Body Keeps the Score by Bessel van der Kolk and Self-Compassion by Kristin Neff provided valuable insights into healing trauma, emotional regulation, and building self-worth. These, along with others listed here, offer deeper exploration of the themes and practices covered in this book and can serve as companions on your journey to emotional freedom and resilience.

Codependency and Emotional Healing

- Beattie, Melody. Codependent No More: How to Stop Controlling Others and Start Caring for Yourself. Harper, 1986.
- Mellody, Pia. Facing Codependence: What It Is, Where It Comes From, How It Sabotages Our Lives. HarperOne, 1989.
- Lancer, Darlene. Codependency for Dummies. Wiley, 2012.

Trauma and Emotional Regulation

- van der Kolk, Bessel. The Body Keeps the Score: Brain, Mind, and Body in the Healing of Trauma. Viking, 2014.
- Siegel, Daniel J. The Developing Mind: How Relationships and the Brain Interact to Shape Who We Are. Guilford Press, 1999.
- Levine, Peter A. Healing Trauma: A Pioneering Program for Restoring the Wisdom of Your Body. Sounds True, 2008.

Attachment Theory

- Bowlby, John. Attachment and Loss, Volume I: Attachment. Basic Books, 1969.
- Ainsworth, Mary D. Salter, and Bowlby, John. Patterns of Attachment: A Psychological Study of the Strange Situation. Psychology Press, 2015.
- Siegel, Daniel J., and Hartzell, Mary. Parenting from the Inside Out: How a Deeper Self-Understanding Can Help You Raise Children Who Thrive. TarcherPerigee, 2013.

Mindfulness and Self-Compassion

- Neff, Kristin. Self-Compassion: The Proven Power of Being Kind to Yourself. William Morrow, 2011.
- Kabat-Zinn, Jon. Wherever You Go, There You Are: Mindfulness Meditation in Everyday Life. Hachette Books, 1994.

Relationship Dynamics and Healthy Boundaries

- Cloud, Henry, and Townsend, John. Boundaries: When to Say Yes, How to Say No to Take Control of Your Life. Zondervan, 1992.
- Tatkin, Stan. Wired for Love: How Understanding Your Partner's Brain and Attachment Style Can Help You Defuse Conflict and Build a Secure Relationship. New Harbinger Publications, 2012.
- Hendrix, Harville, and Hunt, Helen LaKelly. Getting the Love You Want: A Guide for Couples. St. Martin's Griffin, 2007.

Personal Growth and Emotional Freedom

- Brown, Brené. The Gifts of Imperfection: Let Go of Who You Think You're Supposed to Be and Embrace Who You Are. Hazelden, 2010.
- Winfrey, Oprah, and Perry, Bruce D. What Happened to You? Conversations on Trauma, Resilience, and Healing. Flatiron Books, 2021.
- Frankl, Viktor E. Man's Search for Meaning. Beacon Press, 1959.

Made in United States
Orlando, FL
14 June 2025

62120469R00090